Scottish History

Strange but True

Scottish History

Strange but True

John & Noreen Hamilton

Drawings by Clare Buttrick
Digital images by John Hamilton

First published 2016

The History Press
The Mill, Brimscombe Port
Stroud, Gloucestershire, GL5 2QG
www.thehistorypress.co.uk

British Library Cataloguing in Publication Data.
A catalogue record for this book is available from the British Library.

ISBN 978 0 7509 6630 6

Typesetting and origination by The History Press
Printed in Great Britain

Contents

Prologue	7
Who Do We Think We Are?	11
From Bones to Books	30
In the Middle of Things	48
'It Will Pass With a Lass'	81
'A Stony Couch for a Deep Feather Bed'	96
'Yer Fauts I Maun Proclaim'	113
An Age of Change	133
Freedom!	159
'A Dangerous Master'	175
Recommended Reading	189

Prologue

True. It might seem strange to open this book with not one but two assaults on the book's title. We have no problem with 'Strange', but 'True' is a difficult concept. For any event which happens there will be a different version of the event from each different individual who was there, and from every person that hears the story the version will change each time they pass it on. And on and on until someone writes it down and calls it 'History'.

By the way, what about 'HERstory?' How different would our understanding of the past be if it were seen from a woman's point of view?

There are facts, cold hard things – such and such a battle happened in such and such a place on such and such a date and so and so died, but it is the interpretation that is the problem. The experts are hardly in total accord. Archaeologists like solid things, things they can hold in their hand: bones, bullets, swords and pots, they love pots. Historians like documents; it's their job to sort out the lies and damned lies from the merely biased and the misinformed. Neither have any claim to 'Truth'. If a new excavation reveals new clues or if a newly unearthed document casts events in a new light, then the previous conclusions must be changed. All that can be presented is the story of best fit for the information available. If the information changes so must the story. There have been plenty of attempts to change our views, particularly of Scotland's early times, in recent years. Revisionism is rife.

It all comes down to stories. Winston Churchill, amongst others, said, 'History is written by the victors'. But then, Scotland is full of the stories of 'Heroic Failures' (the Jacobite rebellions of the eighteenth century are prime examples).

The great Ulster hero Cuchullin (educated in Scotland) was told that if he took up arms, 'Your life will be short, but your stories will be told forever'. Cuchullin was hardly a victor, though he did get to create a fair bit of mayhem, but his stories are going strong. Perhaps to be included in the collective knowledge of the past, which history is, you don't need a great victory, but you do need a great story.

So that is what we have tried to find – great stories from the area we now call Scotland.

Scotland

The second problem is 'Scotland'. We wrote this book in 2015. In 2014, over 400 years after the Union of the Crowns, Scotland came close to voting for independence. Nationalists narrowly failed to win a 'yes' vote in a referendum. In the 2015 National Election, Scotland voted in fifty-six Scottish Nationalist Party MPs out of fifty-nine seats, leaving the Labour, Liberal and Conservative parties with a single seat each – an overwhelming landslide for the SNP. Seldom has Scotland had such a united pro-independence voice.

For most of history the idea of a single Scottish identity was just that, an idea. An idea born in the medieval power shuffle between Scots, Picts and Britons. Right up to the seventeenth century Highland allegiance was much more to the Lord of the Isles than to some Edinburgh monarch with his airs, graces and trousers. The Borderers offered no allegiance to anyone but to themselves. The Scottish Earls – Hamiltons, Douglases and the like – were merely awaiting their opportunity to step into the king's shoes.

It is not disputed that there were skirmishes with that busy neighbour to the south, but with Scots fighting Picts, clans fighting clans, earls fighting earls, Lowlanders fighting

Highlanders, the state fighting Covenanters and Jacobites fighting Hanoverians, the 'Scots' have always been extremely good at killing 'Scots'. This rings true right up to that most iconic of home derbies, Culloden, where the victorious 'English' army included four Lowland Scots battalions and even some prominent Highland clans such as the Campbells.

We have tried to unpick a little of the origins of the modern Scot, but it is a complex story and it is a story which is constantly evolving.

You may wonder why Al Capone and a student prank in the 1950s turn up in the medieval period and why Saint Columba turns up in the twenty-first century?

We originally intended the book to be a march along Scotland's timeline from prehistory to the modern day. We've had to concede that the past has proved far too complicated for that, far too sinuous. Stories duck and dive and then resurface and dive again. Take, for example, the story of such a solid icon as the Stone of Scone, do we set that at the moment when Edward took it from Scone to London in 1296, or when it was repatriated in 1950 by Glasgow students, or in 1996 when it was returned to Scotland? Or do we go back to when it was moved to Scone from Argyll, or when it came to Argyll from Ireland around AD 500, or when it arrived in Ireland – possibly from the Middle East, possibly in the Bronze Age?

We didn't want to go back to the same story in six different sections of the book. So some stories are told in all their multiplicity where they seem to lie best. Others pop up here and there. Certain themes run right through the ages, others have their particular moment. We have also tried to include recent discoveries, comments and revisions of older stories where they crop up.

A couple of issues have proved unavoidable. The first issue is Scots on the world stage. Scots have made an indelible impression across the globe from early travels in Europe and beyond, to the first footsteps in the New World, to the African National Congress.

The second issue has been the link between Scotland and Ireland. Often their histories are entwined. People have been coming and going across the North Channel since the Ice Age. You may detect a pro-Scottish bias in the text, for which we make no apologies, but this should not be interpreted as anti-English. No reasonable person should be so crass as to fault any person on their place of birth.

However, there is no doubting that through much of Scotland's history England has been the 'Auld Enemy'. We have fought and the numbers tell their story. The population of Scotland has always been about 10 per cent of the population of England. The odds were against us 10/1 all the way. Yet we have held our end up. Be it rugby, football or war, we have had our victories and we celebrate them with some vigour. We also celebrate our heroic failures.

This book is designed as an entertainment: a short romp through the characters, places and events of Scotland's past. We are certainly not academic historians. We have tried to stick, as far as possible, to some version of 'true', but will be as guilty as anyone else of going with a version of the story that we find most convincing – or maybe just the most pleasing.

It is our fervent hope that some of you will find the stories interesting enough to investigate further and set off on a journey, as we have, though the complexity of Scotland's history. Take a look at the past. We can assure you that you will find that it is more complicated, and more fascinating, than you thought.

Who Do We Think We Are?

Drifting continents

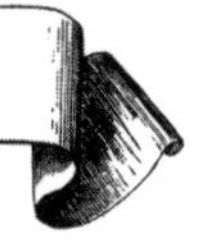

The world is said to be 4.5 billion years old. What is now Scotland and what is now England only became attached about 410 million years ago – about a tenth of the age of the Earth. Before that the two lands were on different continents.

Parts of Scotland, Greenland and North America were formed in the southern hemisphere as part of the continent of Laurentia. Laurentia drifted north, crossing the equator before starting to break up. The North Atlantic Ocean began to form, leaving North America and the Scottish fragment on opposite shores. They still continue to move farther apart. Beds of identical rock can be found on both sides of the ocean, confirming the former union.

Scotland crashed into England, forcing the seabed that lay between them upwards. This explains why the Southern Uplands are largely made up of rocks formed on the bottom of the ocean. Scotland and England became welded together.

On its travels from the south to the north, Scotland was exposed to just about any climatic condition imaginable, from polar cold to baking heat. At times only the highest peaks were above the surface, at others volcanoes poured out smoke and lava, but life still managed to take a hold. Really primitive plants and some of the earliest insects have been found in Aberdeenshire. Later, Scotland was home to numerous species of dinosaur, though fossilised bones are rarely found.

Life could not continue in an unbroken line due to the intervention of ice. Over 2.5 million years glaciers and ice sheets have invaded Scotland in at least five separate ice ages – huge forces carving the rock into landscapes we recognise today.

And it's all still shifting now. The span of human history is but the blink of an eye in geological time, which I have tried to explain in a poem, 'Creation':

And let millennia tick like seconds
And watch the land, to which we tie all symbols of
Solidity and permanence, shift like the sea.
And all our maps and atlases are just snapshots of
Mere Continents which drift, collide,
Spin like so much flotsam in a planet's eddies.
Ebb and flow, rise and fall.

The concept of Scotland

For the vast majority of 10,000 years of human history there was no concept of a single country called 'Scotland'. The first tentative claim to the unity of the land came when Constantine was crowned 'Ri Alban', King of Scots in AD 889, not much more than 1,000 years ago. Before that there were several distinct peoples with distinct languages and cultures.

The last ice age gives us a convenient starting point when discussing the human part of Scotland's story. The ice had effectively wiped the slate clean. There is a common impression that when the ice retreated the land went through a tundra phase and then it blossomed into a wonderful rich, natural wildwood. Then humans arrived and started mucking things up. Given that the melting of the ice was not an overnight event, it is likely that people were here before the forest. There were footprints in the snow.

The question is, where did these first people come from? They came from the ice-free south, but by which route? Some believe that they would have followed the coast. Movement by canoe would have been quicker and easier than travelling through the barren hinterland. Given that the North Sea and the Irish Sea were dry land (or more strictly speaking they would have been largely bog), the coastal route would have led them up the west coast of Ireland and across to the west coast of Scotland. So the first Scottish people came from Ireland. But some people believe it was the other way round. These Mesolithic people were then replaced by Neolithic farmers, though there is evidence that the two cultures existed side-by-side for some time. It is not clear whether the farmers came to Scotland via Ireland or vice versa.

Three nations

The Romans called this place Caledonia; Scotland was still several centuries away. At that time there were three distinct nations: Picts, Goidelic Celts and Bretonic Celts. The Celts are hard to disentangle from their own mythology. Sagas handed down through the oral tradition and eventually written by monks in the seventh to tenth centuries tell of a series of invasions into Ireland bringing Celtic culture with them.

It has been generally accepted that the Celts originated east of the Danube and spread west, becoming the Gauls in what is now France and the Gaels in Ireland and Scotland. They swept in, dominating the lands and imposing their language. The most widely held view is they came in fairly small numbers and took over, living as aristocratic overlords. They may have had a big advantage in the arms race as they could have been the first to have iron-working technology. Archaeologists now tell us that there is no evidence for any such invasion.

It is accepted that the Gaelic-speaking Irish and Highlanders have common cultural roots with a common language, classified as Q-Celtic. These are Goidelic Celts. Scottish Highlanders and Islanders maintained their separate identity, language and distinctive clan structure right up until deliberate attempts were made to destroy the culture after the Battle of Culloden.

By the way, in the early twentieth century it was said that the best spoken English to be found in Britain was in Inverness. This makes sense as many Highlanders at the time would have grown up in entirely Gaelic-speaking communities meaning they would have learned the English language from a textbook in school. They learnt it properly without the sloppiness which comes from centuries of daily misuse.

By the way, Scottish Highlanders were frequently called 'Irish' in the Lowlands, right up until the nineteenth century.

What sort of Celt?

In the south of Scotland the population was represented by an entirely different Celtic culture. These were Bretonic Celts, speaking a separate language, P-Celtic, which was the root for the Welsh, Cornish and Breton languages. These people, divided into several tribes, dominated the Lowlands and Borders. The Kings of Strathclyde ruled from Dumbarton, while the Votadini, in the east, had headquarters at Dun Eidainn, now Edinburgh.

Who were the Picts?

While the Gaels held the west and north, and the Britons held the south, much of the rest was the territory of the Picts. We all know that the Picts were 'the painted people', so called because of their distinctive tattoos, but how much else do we know? 'Pict' was a name given by the Romans – we are not sure what they called themselves.

Roman historian Herodian describes the people in his *History of the Empire after Marcus Book III*:

> Most of the regions of (northern) Britain are marshy, since they are flooded continually by the tides of the ocean; the barbarians are accustomed to swimming or wading through these waist-deep marsh pools; since they go about naked, they are unconcerned about muddying their bodies. Strangers to clothing, they wear ornaments of iron at their waists and throats; considering iron a symbol of wealth, they value this metal as other barbarians value gold. They tattoo their bodies with coloured designs and drawings of all kinds of animals; for this reason they do not wear clothes, which would conceal the decorations on their bodies. Extremely savage and warlike, they are armed only with a spear and a narrow shield, plus a sword that hangs suspended by a belt from their otherwise naked bodies. They do not use breastplates or helmets, considering them encumbrances in crossing the marshes.

This image of the ferocious naked tattooed warrior is pretty much what the name conjures up for most people, yet they occupied much of this country for centuries. The venerable Bede in *Historia Ecclesiastica gentis Anglorum* thinks of them as relatively late arrivals, with this story:

> Picts, putting to sea from Scythia [a vast region stretching from Ukraine to Iran] … came to Ireland and landed on its northern shores. There, finding the nation of the Scots, they begged to be allowed to settle among them … The Scots answered that the island could not contain them both; but 'We can give you good counsel,' said they, 'whereby you may know what to do; we know there is another island, not far from ours, to the eastward, which we often see at a distance, when the days are clear. If you will go thither, you can obtain settlements; or, if any should oppose you, we will help you.

We don't know what language they spoke or much about their culture (we do know that St Columba, a Gaelic speaker, needed a translator when he visited the Picts). One thing they did leave for us was an array of fabulous carved stones. The Picts, however, have not gone away.

The Irish Scots

Scientific company 'ScotlandDNA' have identified a genetic marker as distinctly Pictish, indicating descent from the mysterious tribe. In a sample of over 3,000, the marker, called R1b-S530, was found in 10 percent of Scotsmen. This compares to 0.8 per cent in England and 0.5 per cent in the Republic of Ireland (there is a 3 per cent result in Northern Ireland reflecting the close links with Scotland and the seventeenth-century plantation of Ulster).

The King of Scots

The first recorded mention of 'Scoti' is in a Roman catalogue of the states in the empire compiled around the year AD 314. It lists them alongside Picts and Caledonians as 'barbarian tribes'.

The next reference is by Ammianus Marcellinus in AD 367, '… the Scots, were ranging widely and causing great devastation …'

There is a belief that the word Scoti or Scotti meant 'pirate', but it may be that the word came to have that meaning thanks to the activities of the Scots. It is widely known that these Scots were Irish. The origin goes back to the Middle East. Legend has it that a Greek named Gaythius married a Pharaoh's daughter called Scota. They settled in Spain and later a descendant called Simon Breck brought his Scots to set up a kingdom in Ireland.

Strangely, ScotlandDNA has come up with the revelation that 1 per cent of modern-day Scots have a gene marker which is only found elsewhere in Tuareg and Berber people in the Sahara. Scota's people, perhaps?

The name 'Scot' became associated with the Kingdom of Dalriada, or Dal Riata in the north of Ireland, present-day County Antrim (an area later to be ruled by the MacDonnells from Islay). Centred on Dunseverick, where the remains of a later castle can still be seen, the kingdom started encroaching on territory in Argyll. It was only a short hop across the North Channel. Towards the end of the fifth century, Fergus MacErc and his sons established a permanent settlement on the west coast and extended it to take most of the modern county. The *Annals of Tighernach* record around AD 500, 'Fergus Mor mac Erc, with the nation of Dal Riada, took part of Britain, and died there'.

This has been a long understood story, but some archaeologists have been turning it on its head. They suggest that innovations in crannog and rath (fort) design first appeared in Scotland. Likewise patterns in brooch-making suggest that the movement of ideas, at least, was from Scotland to Ireland and not the other way around. Dr Ewan Campbell, of the University of Glasgow, states, '... if there was a mass migration from Ireland to Scotland, there should be some sign of this in the archaeological record, but there is none.' Whichever way it was, the Scots soon became a force to be reckoned with.

In the ninth century conflict flared between the northern Picts and the southern Britons. The Dalriadan Scots entered the fray as a third contender and somehow carried the day. Dalriadan king Kenneth MacAlpin became King of the Picts. Within fifty years his grandson, Donald, became Ri nan Albanneach – the King of Scots. Scotland had arrived.

By the way, the king here was traditionally known as the King of ***Scots*** rather than the King of ***Scotland***, reflecting an emphasis on community rather than territory.

Romans and walls

There is a popular misconception that the Romans came to Scotland where they met the Picts and were so alarmed that they built a big wall to keep these painted savages out. In fact the Romans were in Scotland for forty-three years before they started building Hadrian's Wall.

In AD 79 Agricola planned the takeover of Caledonia. Five years later he had pushed all the way through to the north east, winning the Battle of Mons Graupius, whose location is a matter of fierce debate. Agricola was then recalled to Rome. The Romans pulled back but did establish themselves in the south of Scotland.

Roman-Britain.org lists sixty-seven sites of Roman forts located throughout Strathclyde, Dumfries and Galloway, Tayside and the Borders. There were substantial settlements, such as Trimontium, on the Eildon Hills just outside Melrose.

A Roman bath house can be seen in Strathclyde Country Park, in Motherwell.

However well Hadrian's Wall worked at keeping the Picts in, it certainly didn't keep the Romans out. In a conspicuous effort to expand northwards they built the Antonine Wall, nearly a hundred miles further north, twenty years after Hadrian's.

As the Roman Empire crumbled the Picts rampaged over the wall and the remaining Romano-Britons needed help in keeping them at bay.

The English

We generally think that the Angles and Anglo-Saxons who created Angle Land – England, were not part of Scotland's historical landscape, but they did play their part. These Germans were invited into England to act as mercenaries to face down the incursions from the north. Once they became established in Angleland they did try to expand their territories northward.

King Ida of Bernicia established an Anglian Kingdom north of Hadrian's Wall in the Tweed Valley, battling the resident Britons. Angles moved into Dumfriesshire and Galloway. They met and defeated Dalriadans when they made a move into Argyll. They faced up to the Picts, who finally defeated them in AD 685.

> By the way, the Gaelic word for an Englishman, a Sassenach, derives, more or less, from Saxon-ach, (Scots are Albannach, Irish are Eirannach).

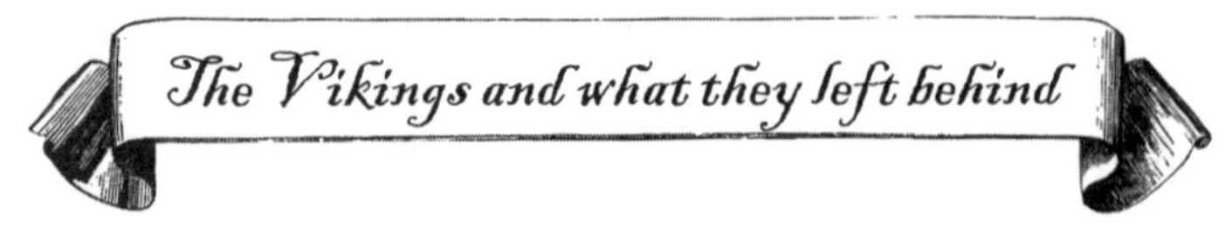

The Vikings and what they left behind

Officially the first Viking excursion to Britain was in AD 793 when they attacked the monastery on Lindisfarne, followed by attacks on monks on Iona and Rathlin Island. Of course, they must have been here before – how else would they have known which targets to pick? The Norse handed over control of the Hebrides to Scotland in the treaty of Perth on 2 July 1266. They were around after that and they did leave a lot behind including a lot of Norse words, Norse place names and quite a lot of Norse genetics.

> **By the way, we should remember that the word 'Viking' is derived from a root meaning 'sea raider or pirate'. No one from Scandinavia should be called a Viking if they are peacefully going about their business.**

The greatest Scottish Viking hunter

Somerled was born around 1113, supposedly from a noble Gaelic family related to the Kings of Dalriada, however new DNA evidence casts some doubt.

Somerled is the great Gaelic hero. The Macdonald and other clans claim him as their forefather, but his Celtic credentials are in some doubt. It was accepted that it was likely that his mother was a Norwegian. Recent DNA studies reveal that his Y chromosome, which comes through the male line, was distinctly Norse.

Professor Bryan Sykes of Oxford University studied the DNA of men from three clans who all claim descent from Somerled: MacDonalds, MacDougalls and MacAllisters. A significant percentage of them carry a Y chromosome from a common ancestor which is rare everywhere except Norway.

Somerled, it appears, was Norse on both sides of his family. Given that it is not doubted that he married a Norwegian, Ragnhild, daughter of Olaf the Red, King of Mann, this means that their descendants, the line of the Lords of the Isles, are pretty much Viking.

By the way, Professor Sykes also calculates that Somerled has 500,000 living descendants, making him second only to Genghis Khan (who has a staggering 16 million).

The Normans

William the Conqueror lived up to his name in 1066. He did have a crack at Scotland in 1072 but was 'sent hameward'. The Normans did arrive and they did make a huge impact on Scottish history.

The Conqueror's son became Henry I of England. He married 'Good Queen Maud' who was the daughter of Malcolm Canmore, King of Scotland. Her younger brother, David, grew up in the Norman court, learnt their ways and customs and made Norman friends. In 1124 he returned to Scotland as King David I. He brought friends with him.

He awarded many of these Norman sons Scottish lands and titles. He adopted many aspects of the Norman feudal system, creating royal burgs, now boroughs (Berwick and Roxboro were the first, reflecting David's love for the Borders area). He established, or re-established, abbeys and brought in European religious orders.

King David's Norman pals quickly became part of the elite of Scotland. Their French surnames became 'Scotified' and these names crop up again and again in Scottish history. They include: Comyn, Balliol, Graham, Bisset, Boyle, Corbett, Hay, Kinnear, Fraser, Montgomery, Boswell, Menzies and, significantly, Bruce. The Stewarts also arrived as part of the Norman influx; their family name was Fitz Alan (the 'Stewart' came from the title 'Steward of Scotland'). They were not strictly Norman; they were Bretons. The Bretons were Britons who arrived in the north of France in the fourth century. While they might have arrived directly from south-west England, we will see that Britons from the Lothians and Borders moved south in the preceding centuries. Maybe the Stewarts do have a longer Scottish history than was thought. We didn't say this was going to be straightforward.

> **By the way, a recent study revealed that 15 per cent of men with the surname Stewart have genes that link them to the royal line.**

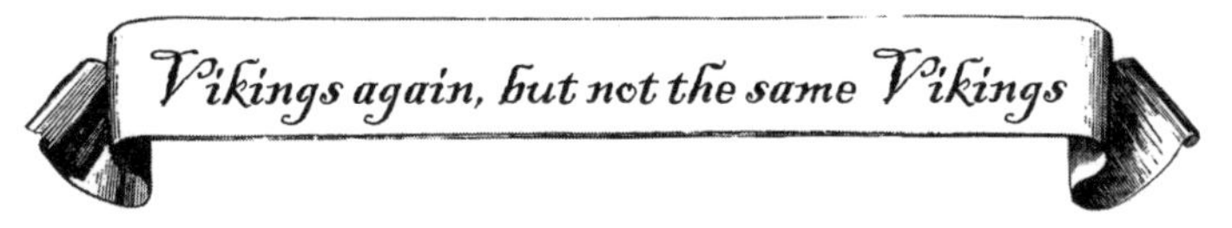

Norman blood was now added to the Scottish mix, but it wasn't French; it was Scandinavian blood again. 'Norman' is a corruption of 'Northmen' or 'Norsemen'. In the early tenth century a force of Scandinavians, under a commander called Rollo, invaded what is now France. The local king, Charles the Simple, was not so daft as to think he could defeat these fearsome Vikings. Instead he offered them land. The Northmen could settle along the north coast and provide a buffer against any further incursions. Normandy came into being and, just a few generations later, the Normans came to Britain.

However, recent genetic research reveals that these Vikings were distinct from the Vikings settling in the north and west. While those who settled the Northern Isles and had such an influence on the west coast were largely from Norway, the Normandy settlers were of Danish stock. The Danes, it appears, have more DNA in common with their Anglo-Saxon neighbours to the south than with the Norwegians.

By the way, Norman genetics would have been a mixture of Scandinavian and French as the majority of the settlers were men. They found themselves local wives.

Along with Normans came Bretons and Flemish. The Flemish were to have great influence on Scottish woollen textiles, particularly in the Borders. The abbeys were involved in the production; Melrose Abbey had over 25,000 sheep at one point.

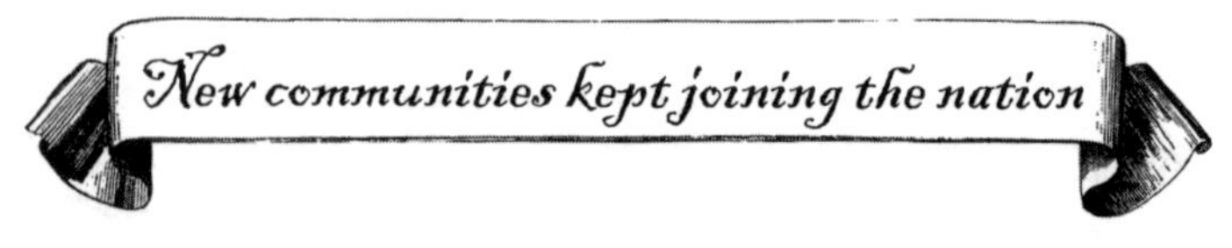

New communities kept joining the nation

The nineteenth century saw an influx of Jews fleeing pogroms in Russia, Lithuania, Estonia, Latvia and Poland, with a second wave from Germany and Poland fleeing Hitler in the 1930s. A substantial community from Lithuania became established in Lanarkshire, working in the coal mines.

At the start of the twentieth century came the Italians. What Scottish childhood would be complete without Italian ice cream and Italian fish and chips and without the sound of the 'Tally Van'? How many famous Scots have Italian roots – Paulo

Nutini, Charlene Spiteri, Peter Capaldi, Lena Zavaroni, to name a few.

Chinese, Indian, Bangladeshi and Pakistani immigrants followed. Where would our national cuisine be without them?

> By the way, chicken tikka masala, one of the most popular dishes in the UK, was invented in Glasgow. Ali Ahmed Aslam of the Shish Mahal Restaurant in Park Road had an awkward customer who complained that his chicken tikka was 'too dry'. Ali added a tin of condensed tomato soup and the new dish was born. In 2015, local MP Mohammed Sarwar launched a campaign to have chicken tikka masala recognised as an official Glasgow dish, in the same way that Dundee cake and Arbroath smokies are acknowledged.

The Irish, again

The Irish have been coming and going forever. In the nineteenth century there was an established pattern of Irish workers arriving to work the harvests and returning home. In the 1840s the situation changed. In Ireland (and in Scotland, particularly the Highlands) the potato harvest failed (again). This is generally known as the 'Great Famine', but in Ireland it is now more acceptable to call it the 'Great Hunger' since there was no shortage of food. Ireland was exporting large quantities of oats, barley, meat and butter. The food was there but the poor had no access to it.

Those that could raise the price of a ticket headed for America. Poorer folk could manage a ticket for the boat to Scotland (6*d* on the boat to Greenock). For the poorest there was no escape at all. Like all the other immigrant groups they encountered considerable hostility and like the other groups they initially kept to themselves, reluctant to assimilate. Remnants of that isolation remain, but as each community stays longer in their new home the more barriers come down and the more they merge with the Scottish nation.

> **By the way, more Irish moved to Scotland in the late 1840s than Scots and English settlers during the entire project of the Plantation of Ulster in the seventeenth century. The Irish in Scotland had nothing like the political and cultural impact of the plantation settlers. The Irish were coming in at the very lowest rung of society while many of the planters were moving in as landowners.**

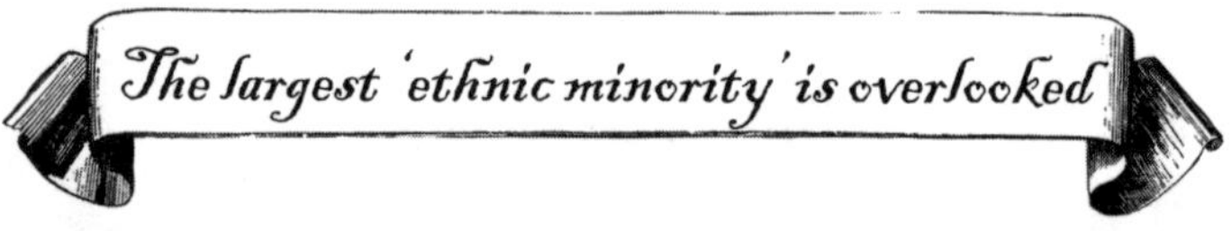

The largest source of immigrants to Scotland is the most overlooked. This group made up 1.5 per cent of the Scottish population in 1841, rising to 4 per cent in 1921. And the influx continues. In the most recent census they made up 7.88 per cent compared with 5.02 per cent of every other ethnic group put together.

Some 459,486 Scottish residents were born in that country, making it the greatest source of immigration into Scotland. That country is England. The Oxford University Migrant Observatory noted, 'If people from England, Wales and Northern Ireland were counted as immigrants, Scotland's population (of immigrants) would rise to nearly 18 per cent, a higher proportion than the USA.'

Of course, we are, up to the present, a United Kingdom and to be fair there are 708,872 Scots-born citizens living in England. Perhaps we are a united nation after all.

Recent years have seen numbers of Eastern Europeans arriving, just as they did in the nineteenth century. They have met some hostility too. At the time of writing the EU is discussing ways to diffuse a 'migrant crisis'. A poll, carried out by Oxford University Migration Observatory in 2014, suggested that Scots were (slightly) more welcoming to immigrants than the rest of the UK.

So who are the Scots?

We have seen that the earliest settlers came either from western Europe along a coastal route, or overland from central Europe. Bronze Age people, possibly, came from Egypt or the Middle East. Iron Age Celts came from east of the Danube. The Scots came from Ireland. The Romans and the Anglo-Saxons came and went, but will have left some DNA behind. The Normans brought more Norse along with some French blood. The Bretons and Flemish came with them. The English have always been among us.

The nineteenth century saw the arrival of more Irish plus Russian and Baltic Jews, Polish, Lithuanians and Italians. The twentieth brought Chinese, Indians, Bengladeshis and Pakistanis. The twenty-first is bringing us more East Europeans and some Africans.

Scotland, at the point that Scotland as a concept became at all recognisable, was an amalgam of three nations. From that mongrel start Scotland has become more and more of a 'rainbow nation'. In the 2014 independence referendum no attempt was made to establish any element of Scottish ethnicity. If you were resident in Scotland you had your say.

From Bones to Books

We have no documents from our early history to help us establish the facts. We have to read the bones and the stones. What the bones and stones say is not always clear.

The oldest toilet

The Toilet Guru (yes, there is one, he has a website) claims that the top candidate for the world's first recorded indoor toilet is at Skara Brae on the Orkney mainland. Archaeologists are, as usual, not prepared to give a definite answer, but they are not denying that the drainage systems in some of the buildings could be the first lavatories.

Skara Brae was a remarkable discovery. It was naturally preserved under sand for thousands of years until in 1851 a storm blew away enough sand to reveal the secret. A 5,000-year-old village was unearthed in exceptional condition. The stone rooms give us a real sense of what life might have been like in the Stone Age; they were equipped with beds, seats and dressers.

We think of the islands as being remote and hard to reach, but in the past the sea was the highway. Places like Shetland, Orkney and the Hebrides were not on the edge: they were at the centre. Neolithic constructions such as the Stones of Stenness and the Ring of Brodgar on Orkney and the Callanish Stones on Lewis (all older than Stonehenge) tell the story of a well-organised and disciplined society.

The writer and historian Brian Aldiss said that, 'the degree of civilisation can be measured by the distance man puts between himself and his own excrement'. Why should that sophisticated Orcadian society not invent the loo?

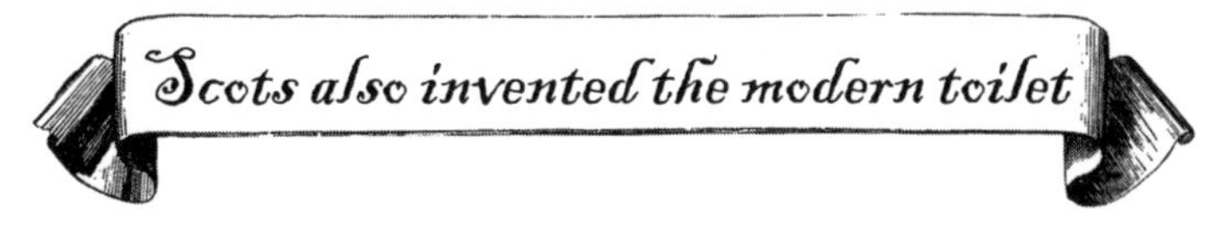

Scots also invented the modern toilet

It is commonly thought that Thomas Crapper invented the flushing toilet. The Toilet Guru poo-poos this idea. The first flush was created by Englishman Sir John Harrington, a courtier of Elizabeth I. He was also famous for writing bawdy verse. It was not until 1777 that an Edinburgh watchmaker, Alexander Cummings, patented the design that we still use today. The critical element was the 'S bend' which traps water below the bowl, preventing smells drifting up from the pipes beneath.

Other inventions

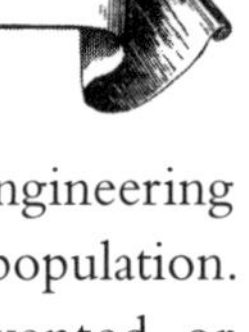

Scotland's contributions to the worlds of science, engineering and even cuisine have outweighed the size of our population. Among the things Scots can claim to have invented, or discovered, are: adhesive postage stamps; anaesthetics; antiseptics; advertising films; the agricultural reaping machine; Bakelite; Brownian motion; chemical bonds; chicken tikka masala; the cure for scurvy; the decimal point; fax machines; flailing machines; golf; the historical novel; hypodermic syringes; iron bridges; the Kelvin scale of temperature; logarithms; marmalade; Mackintosh raincoats; microwave ovens; paraffin; the percussion cap; penicillin; pneumatic tyres; postcards; quinine; radar defence; refrigerators; the steam engine; the steam-hammer; sulphuric acid; tarmacadam; the telephone; the telegraph; the television; and, of course, the deep-fried Mars bar.

By the way, the Neolithic cairn on Orkney, Maeshowe, was raided by Vikings. While sheltering from a snowstorm they amused themselves by inscribing graffiti on the walls. Some of it is very rude. The inscriptions include a reference to Ragnarr Loftbrok, the character fictionalised in the recent TV series 'Vikings'.

Scottish Frankenstein

A 2001 excavation on the Isle of South Uist unearthed an astounding mystery. At Cladh Hallan two skeletons were discovered, presumed to be from the Bronze Age. The skeletons were from a man and a woman, both buried in a foetal position. So far, so good. It was when they started to examine the bones that things started to go awry. One skeleton with clearly a female torso appeared to have the skull of a man. When the DNA and other test results started coming in things got really weird. Not only did she have a male skull, but her arm also belonged to someone else! The three people weren't even closely related.

The male skeleton was no less surprising, bones in his skull, neck and torso belong to three different people. Stranger still, isotopic dating showed that the male mummy is made from people who died a few hundred years apart. The skull on the female turned out to be 50–100 years older than her torso.

Further test results showed that the bones had spent some time in a peat bog before being retrieved and re-buried. It seemed that the natural processes in bogs whereby organic material is preserved were being harnessed in a form of a mummification process. 'Mummification has been surprisingly widespread throughout world history, but this is the first time we've seen clear evidence that it was employed during the Bronze Age on the British Isles,' said University College London archaeologist Mike Parker Pearson. The weird couple were labelled by the press as the 'Scottish Frankenstein Mummies'.

In peat bogs the rotting of most organic material is inhibited, however this doesn't apply to bone because of its calcium content. This explains why most bog bodies look like saggy leather sacks. They are literally spineless. In the Cladh Hallan case it appears that the bodies were 'bog mummified' for long enough for the flesh to be preserved, but not so long as to let the bones decay. The fact that the bones, within each section, were still attached to each other indicates that there must have been flesh present when they were moved to the burial site.

So it appears that different parts of six mummies of different ages were reassembled as two bodies and given a proper Bronze Age burial. The question is, why?

There are theories, but no answers. The archaeologist Mike Parker Pearson of UCL suggests, 'The mixing of remains could have been designed to combine different ancestries or families into a single line of descent. At the time, land rights would have depended on ancestral claims, so perhaps having ancestors around "in the flesh" was the prehistoric equivalent of a legal document.'

Professor Terry Brown, of Manchester University, suggests that maybe they weren't too good at mummy management: 'Maybe the head dropped off and they got another head to stick on.'

Another possibility is that the merging was deliberate, to create a symbolic ancestor that literally embodied traits from multiple lineages. We wondered if it could be that someone came across a cache of bog bodies, which they had nothing to do with, and just did the decent thing by giving the bits they could find a proper burial.

There are facts in the fantasies

By the time we get to the Iron Age we have a new resource – oral history. Myths (or are they legends?) gathered into epic sagas were passed down through generations by word of mouth. Each generation added its own embellishments so that the heroes got more heroic, the villains got more villainous and the underlying current of magic got more, well, magical. There have always been those who have argued that beneath the fantastical veneer lay real stories about real people, making these 'legends' (stories with a factual basis) as opposed to 'myths' (stories with a fictional basis). Others have scoffed, dismissing the sagas as mere fantasies. In recent years more and more archaeologists have been reviewing the material and finding, more and more, that the stories and the physical evidence support each other, and vice versa.

Hero in the mountains

The Irish sagas are particularly rich, but they are full of relevance for Scotland. The Cuillin mountains on the Isle of Skye are named after the Irish legend Cuchullin, demonstrating how close the links across the North Channel were even 2,000 years ago. Cuchullin is a leading figure in the 'Ulster Cycle' which described events that happened 'around the time of Christ'. This is supported by recent archaeology. The central location of the saga is the fort of Emain Macha which has long been identified as Navan Fort just outside Armagh. Dendrochronology studies (tree-ring dating) of the centre post of an Iron Age roundhouse excavated at Navan give a date of just after 100 BC.

In the stories Cuchullin, already quite successful in martial arts, comes to Scotland to further his education. He attends a university of violence on the Isle of Skye under the tutelage of the warrior queen Sciatach. While there he meets Ferdia, his best buddy (until Cuchullin slaughters him). He also gets involved in a skirmish with a second warrior queen, Aoife. The two find themselves in a clinch where they stare into each other's eyes. Shortly afterwards, Aoife finds herself pregnant and Cuchullin returns to Ireland. Their boy, Connla, visits Ireland years later and is challenged on the beach by his father.

Following instructions left by Cuchullin for his infant son, Connla refuses to give his name or to back down. Cuchullin murders his own son. It didn't pay to get close to this man. His potential Scottish lineage didn't last long.

In the later cycle of Fionn MacCumhaill (Finn MacCool) stories, in some versions of the story of Fionn's pursuit of Diarmud, who had run off with his wife Grainne, the events end dramatically in Glen Etive. Local place names seem to support this.

Tales of Cuchullin and Finn MacCool featured strongly in West Highland oral traditions until recent times.

An epic fake

In the years from 1761 Scots poet James MacPherson, from Ruthven near Kingussie, published translations of ancient Gaelic manuscripts. The stories were written in the voice of Ossian, telling the tales of his father, Fingal. Clearly these were tales related to the stories of Fionn MacCumhaill and Oisin, his son.

The collection of poems was very successful and was translated into several languages, but there was doubt from the start. Samuel Johnson described MacPherson as 'a mountebank, a liar and a fraud'. It does have to be said that Johnson also described the Gaelic language as 'the rude speech of a barbarous people'.

It is now accepted that while finding inspiration amongst songs and scraps of ancient literature, MacPherson largely made Ossian up himself. The collection has been described as 'the most successful literary falsehood in modern history'. It is still an impressive piece of work.

The Welsh Scots

When I first moved to Peebles in the 1980s I heard it said that names like Peebles and Penicuik were Welsh. It was commonly known. However, a little research quickly turned this on its head.

When the Romans came to Scotland, the tribe occupying an area equivalent to much of the Borders and Lothians were called the 'Votadini' by the Romans. They were Bretonic Celt, very distinct from the Gaelic Celts of the Highlands. After a few skirmishes they decided, as so many peoples across Europe had, that getting on with the Romans was the better option.

The Romans, impressed by their warrior skills, offered them extensive territory farther south and to the west of Roman Britain. The job was to keep the locals quiet and resist Irish pirates. The Votadini, or Gododdin as they called themselves, took up the challenge.

Moving to North Wales, they had a huge influence on local language and culture. Contacts between the two regions were maintained, as indicated by the fact that the best history of the tribe was written by the Welsh poet Aneirin. The poem 'Y Gododdin' (the date of which is uncertain, but the events described are reckoned to be late sixth–early seventh centuries) tells stories of the Gododdin partying in Dun Eidyn (Edinburgh) for a year before heading out to a battle at Catraech – which is interpreted as Catterick. The force includes fighting men from different southern Scottish regions, as well as men from North Wales. The battle was a disaster for the allied troops. 'Y Gododdin' also contains possibly the first known reference to King Arthur.

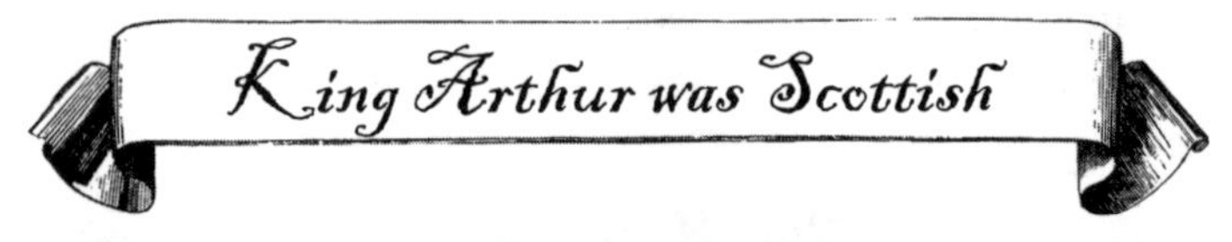

King Arthur was Scottish

What Wales, the West Country and Southern Scotland had in common was Bretonic Celt ancestry, the true 'British' in fact. Aneirin's poetry reveals that there were not just cultural but also political links between these areas. It is not surprising that such a good story as the hero warrior King Arthur should travel about a bit.

Borders folklore has long owned Arthur and, more particularly, Merlin. Arthur and his knights lie in a secret cave in the Eildon Hills waiting only for the signal to rise and defend Britain again. Should you stumble upon the cave you will be presented with the choice between a horn and a sword – 'woe betide the coward who picks up the horn before the sword'. You have been warned!

Merlin, too, may be trapped in a cave in the Border hills or he may be buried at Merlin's Grave in Merlindale, would you believe? (The place names are a bit of a giveaway, take Arthur's Seat in Edinburgh, for example.) Merlin died by 'falling, stabbing and drowning' as he himself predicted. Chased by shepherds, he tumbled into the River Tweed where he was impaled on a structure for salmon fishing, trapped underwater, and drowned.

These associations with Merlin and Arthur are not a new discovery. In the thirteenth century Thomas the Rhymer mentions Merlin's Grave (at the site commemorated by a thorn tree today) in a prophesy:

> When Tweed and Powsail [Burn] meet at Merlin's Grave
> Scotland and England shall one King have.

Naturally, on the date James VI became James I of England, a huge flood in the named river and burn inundated the grave.

Further local tradition tells of Merlin's conversion to Christianity. After leading a pagan army against the Christian forces of Strathclyde and losing badly, he was baptised by Saint Kentigern. The altar stone used in the ceremony is kept in Stobo Kirk (near Peebles) as proof and a stained-glass window celebrates the event.

This Christian element may be a later addition to the Bretonic tales, but then so is just about everything we know about Arthur and Merlin. The shining armour, the sword in the stone, the round table, the Lady in the Lake, Lancelot, Guinevere and Mordred are all later add-ons. Geoffrey of Monmouth, in the twelfth century, was influential but it was Thomas Mallory's fifteenth-century *Le Morte D'Arthur* that crystallised the popular notions of King Arthur.

The truth of Arthur's origins lies in a mosaic of Bretonic tribes warring with each other and with Picts and Angles, overlaid by folklore and scant documents along with archaeological remains (much of it unexplored). Alistair Moffat's 1995 book *Arthur and the Lost Kingdoms* explores all this in depth. The case for a Scottish Arthur stands strong.

The Lord of the Isles

Somerled (pronounced Sorley) has gone down in history as the great Gaelic Viking hunter. Legend has it that when a Viking war party landed in Argyll, Somerled was fishing. He was sent for but refused to move until he caught the salmon he was angling for (being a keen fisherman I find this entirely understandable). Thankfully he did land the fish and headed for the battle. He struck down the first attacker he came across, split open his chest and ripped out his heart. He charged into the fray brandishing Norwegian offal.

Somerled's grandfather, Gilledomman of the Isles, had been defeated by the Norse and exiled to Ireland. When he was a child, Somerled's more immediate family was also expelled from their home and sent to Ireland. His father Gillebride raised an army of 500 and returned to Morvern to regain their lands, but was beaten off and killed. Around 1135 Somerled led a successful rebellion which cleared Norse control from Morvern, Lochaber and much of Argyll. He became the Thane of Argyll.

In 1158 he took on the unpopular King of Mann, Godred II or Godfrey the Black. The Kingdom of Mann controlled much of the sea between Britain and Ireland. It was a Norse kingdom, paying homage to the Kings of Norway. In a decisive sea battle using galleys equipped with rudders, the latest in naval technology, he defeated Godred.

Somerled declared himself '*Ri Innse Gall*' or Lord of the Isles, effectively setting up an autonomous state, the Lordship of the Isles, which was independent of both Norway and Scotland. This institution was to last for three centuries, ending in 1493, when John MacDonald was forced to forfeit his land and titles to James IV (he had been plotting with the English King Edward VI to invade Scotland).

By the way, the title 'The Lord of the Isles' still exists. The current holder is Prince Charles. Charles is also the Duke of Rothesay, Earl of Carrick, Baron of Renfrew and High Steward of Scotland.

Scots were in America before Columbus

It is recorded in the *Saga of Erik the Red* that Leif Ericsson discovered America around AD 1,000 by accident when he was blown off course on a trip to Greenland. He called it Vinland on account of the berries he found.

Four years later Thorfinn Karisefni led a new expedition to explore this promised land of wine. Among a crew of around 160 on three ships were two Scots. They were slaves – a man named Haki and a woman named Hekja. They had a reputation as fast runners and so were landed with instructions to make their way along the shore, while the rest of the expedition followed offshore in the safety of their ships. The couple were being used as bait so that any unfriendly natives would reveal themselves. None appeared so the Norse came ashore. The expedition did later encounter hostiles, but did not find much in the way of 'wine berries'. After three years they abandoned the continent.

King Haakon died twice

In the thirteenth century a fight was brewing. King Haakon IV of Norway and Alexander II of Scotland were ambitious men; both were keen to stamp their authority over the islands and the seaway between Scotland and Ireland. Battles had long been fought between Scots and Norse but there had been no decisive fixture. A showdown was called for.

Haakon mustered his forces in Orkney and sailed down though the Hebrides, reaffirming allegiances and gathering forces as he went. By the time he reached the Clyde he was said to have up to 120 ships and 20,000 men. A massive force. Alexander knew he had no chance in an open sea battle. He drew out negotiations with Haakon's envoys and waited until his secret weapon was deployed – the Scottish weather!

On 1 October the storm hit. It was sudden and violent. Haakon's fleet was shattered and many ships were driven ashore. The next morning a bedraggled Haakon was ashore with about 1,000 men near Largs. It was then that Alexander's men attacked. It was not a huge victory for either side, but it was effectively the last great battle between Scotland and Norway and the end of Viking power in the area.

Haakon escaped back to Orkney. Or did he? Local tradition had it that he died in the battle and was buried nearby. 'Haakon's Tomb' is a well-known landmark in the town of Largs. Closer examination reveals that the monument is actually a Neolithic chambered tomb and was built around 4,000 years before the Battle of Largs.

The other story tells that Haakon made it back to Orkney, where he died two months later. After three years Haakon's son, Magnus IV, relinquished his claim to the Hebrides and the Isle of Man for 4,000 silver merks in the 'Treaty of Perth'.

By the way, when a monument commemorating the battle was planned for Largs, the planners made no decision as to how high it was going to be. Built in 1912, the Pencil Monument is a simple round tower. The builders put the money for the roof aside and kept fundraising while the tower was under construction. They kept building as long as the money kept coming in.

It's all in the Monk's work

It was the monks who, in the seventh–tenth centuries, wrote down the stories that had been in the oral tradition for the best part of 1,000 years. The documents concerned are the Annals, and are intended to be the reliable history of the time. In some cases the documents are compilations of earlier documents or collections of information harvested from them, sometimes spanning centuries. The *Annals of the Four Masters* record events from the earliest times up to the seventeenth century. They are the most authentic records we have of the early period, and much of what is known of the so-called Dark Ages depends on these books.

The 200ft woman

The past throws up some truly unbelievable stories. But what can we believe? Surely documentary evidence is helpful, but history being what it is, it is advisable to find more than one source for any story. This is a dictum we have stuck to religiously in compiling this book.

This story has not two, but four sources. Given that the event occurred in what we call the Dark Ages, when documents are very few and hard evidence of any kind is hard to come by, this level of agreement is astounding. Surely this must be fact.

The story is of a woman washed up on the shores of Scotland. She had very pale skin, long hair and was nearly 200ft tall! There are slight discrepancies in the measurement, suggesting that it wasn't all just copied from a single origin. It would make no sense to change a measurement by a few feet.

The *Annals of Ulster* (AD 891) records: 'The sea threw up a woman in Scotland. She was a hundred and ninety-five feet in height; her hair was seventeen feet long; the finger of her hand was seven feet long, and her nose seven feet. She was all as white as swan's down.' This is very similar to the story which appears in the *Annals of the Four Masters* (AD 891) but with a different length of hair.

The *Annals of Innisfallen* (AD 906) says, 'A great woman was cast upon the shore of Scotland in this year. She was a hundred and ninety-two feet in length; the length of her hair was sixteen feet; the fingers of her hand were six feet long, and her nose was six. Her body was as white as swan's down, or sea foam.'

Chronicon Scotorum (AD 900) which admits that it had copied the story from the *Annals of Tigernach*, notes, 'A great woman was cast ashore by the sea in Scotland; her length 192ft; there were six feet between her two breasts; the length of her hair was 15ft; the length of a finger on her hand was six feet; the length of her nose was 7ft. As white as swan's down or the foam of the wave was every part of her.'

Make of it what you will.

In the Middle of Things

The Dark Ages slid into what we call the Middle Ages or Medieval period. The loss of the term 'dark' would suggest some form of enlightenment. The period did include huge advancements in philosophy, science and theology, but also its fair share of mayhem and bloodshed.

Forts, Duns and Raths, defensive structures of various types, had littered the landscape from at least the Iron Age. It was in the Middle Ages that castle building really took off.

Location, location, location

The design of a castle is one thing, but most critical is 'location, location, location'. The site is vital both in the sense of the strategic importance and in the use of the local geography. Stirling Castle is a good example. It is built at the first place where the River Forth could be forded and where building a bridge was a reasonable proposition. The bridge (here from around 1500) was the lowest crossing point on the river until colossal Victorian imaginations contemplated the construction of something as impressive as the Forth Bridge.

An army intending to proceed north or south could not pass to the east of Stirling. To the west today lies hospitable farm land, flat fields and hedges; in the past this area, the Carse of Stirling, was anything but hospitable. This was a vast swamp, up to 18ft deep in places – a maze of dark pools and sodden bog.

Small bands of outlaws, such as Rob Roy MacGregor's men, might have been able to pick a cautious way through. For a marching army it would be a nightmare and for cavalry an impossibility, until it was drained by the Kames of Blairdrummond in a project that started in 1766 and took nearly eighty years to complete. An army could not pass to the west of Stirling.

Stirling was of critical strategic importance and this was not lost on the kings of Scotland. Here a castle was needed and geology provided the perfect foundation: 350 million years ago molten volcanic rock cooled and, after the icy hand of successive glaciers had left their mark, here was the perfect castle site. Three sides are steep cliff and the only approach is a long, slow slope. The stones and mortar are just an embellishment.

Quite how early this was used as a military base is not known, but it was too good to have been missed. By the time of the first written record (Alexander I opened a chapel here in 1110) there had certainly been a succession of structures here, building and rebuilding on the same spot as design ideas and technology changed. If the location was right it made no sense to move.

Picked by a donkey

Quite why William, the third 'Thane of Cawdor', decided to up sticks and abandon an earlier castle, of which there is now little trace, is not known. However, when he came to choose a new spot he wanted more than a survey of the area – he wanted mystical intervention.

The information as to how to engage spiritual support came to him in a dream. Around 1350 he loaded gold on to the back of a donkey and set it free to roam. All day he followed the beast until eventually, as dusk began to fall, it settled itself down beneath a small tree. This was the spot for the new castle, dictated by unknown mystical forces.

It is not clear what happened to the donkey, but the tree now had a magical quality. The tree was not removed; rather the castle was built around it. Had William had the foresight to have created a courtyard for it the tree might have survived, but he built it into a cellar. With the lack of light it didn't last long. Curiously, the cellar, named the Hawthorn Room, is still there and the remains of the tree can still be seen. Recent research reveals that it was a holly and not a hawthorn and that it died in 1153. Still, its magical properties were reckoned to save the castle on more than one occasion.

The first war

Scotland as an entity was just coming together. On the Scottish throne was Constantine II; his predecessor, Donald I, was the first to be King of Scots rather than King of the Picts.

Æthelstan was similarly among the first to be called the King of the English. He was keen on establishing his might, subduing the Welsh kings and turning to Scotland in AD 934. He was shadowed by a naval fleet. He roundly defeated Owen of Strathclyde and kept marching north. He made it all the way to Caithness. There were skirmishes along the way. Dunnottar Castle, near Stonehaven, held him up when it successfully withstood a month-long siege. Ultimately, he turned south again without any decisive battles taking place. The *Annals of Clanmacnoise* state that 'the Scottishmen compelled [him] to return without any great victory'.

He had, however, done enough to impress. Constantine travelled south with him, effectively acknowledging Æthelstan as his overlord.

Æthelstan was to get his decisive battle a few years later when Constantine, in alliance with Owen of Strathclyde and Olaf Gruthfrithson, King of Dublin, made a retaliatory strike into England. They were destroyed by Æthelstan's forces at the Battle of Brunanburh. It was known for generations afterwards as the 'Great Battle'.

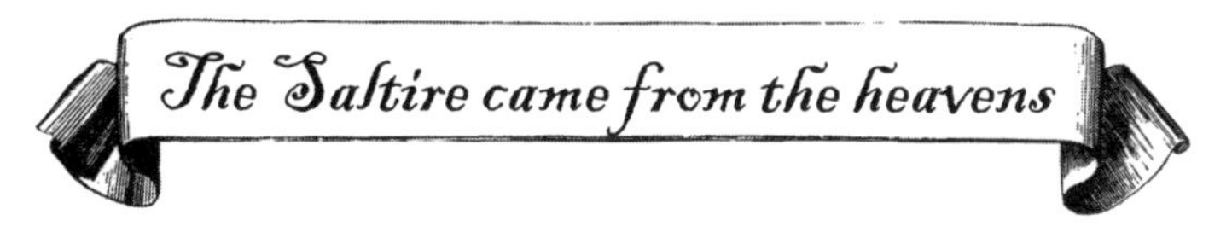

The Saltire came from the heavens

The story of the origins of the village of Athelstaneford in East Lothian, and the origins of the adoption of the Saltire as a national flag, involves a different Æthelstan, possibly one recorded as King of the Angles and based in East Anglia.

This story set in AD 832, 100 years before the other Æthelstan's Scottish adventure, pits an English king, Athelstan, against a Pictish king, Angus. Angus, on the eve of battle, prayed and was answered by a vision of St Andrew. Bearing in mind the knowledge that St Andrew was crucified on an X-shaped cross, the following morning Angus could clearly discern the shape of the diagonal cross etched in white clouds against the blue background. The Saltire was born and Scotland had its patron saint.

Suffice to say that, with the saint's blessing, Angus won the day. They caught up with the retreating Athelstan at a ford. His head was mounted on a pole and Athelstaneford had its name.

The 13 contenders for King of Scotland

If you asked the proverbial man on the street to name a king of Scotland, he might well mention 'James' – there were eight of them after all (if you count the Old Pretender), with Jamie Saxt (James VI of Scotland and James I of England) being the most memorable. Some might remember Kenneth McAlpin, but he only claimed to be King of the Picts. The first King of Scots, Donald, is hardly remembered at all. We think that the overwhelming vote for the best known king would be Robert the Bruce. Yet he was a Norman.

Bruce's ancestor was Robert de Bruis, a Norman knight from near Cherburg. He landed with William the Conqueror (1066 and all that). He took an English wife who was a distant relative of King William I, 'The Lion'.

By the way, when Prince William becomes King William V of England, he will need to bear in mind that he should be William VI in Scotland, as we had our William I, back in the twelfth century.

De Bruis's son came to Scotland and aided King David, and was awarded land in Annandale. He later served as a commander in the English army. Another four Robert the Bruces later, we come to the well-known one.

There was a succession crisis in 1291. Alexander III fell off his horse and died. His only surviving daughter, Margaret, the Maid of Norway, didn't make it to her eighth birthday. The throne was vacant. There were thirteen claimants; among them was Robert the Bruce from Annandale.

The extraordinary step of inviting Edward I, King of England to decide on the winner was taken. He was anxious to find someone he could easily control. He ignored Bruce and chose John Baliol. This was not to everyone's liking.

Fourteen blood-stained years later Bruce was crowned Robert I of Scotland. Balliol had abdicated and was in exile in France (the original king o'er the water).

Robert Bruce, hero of Bannockburn (one of the few great home wins against England) became ingrained in the Scottish consciousness.

Recent years have seen many argue that Scot William Wallace should be celebrated as the great hero of the period (the movie, however far off the facts, did him no harm), rather than the Norman, Bruce. But then Bruce did keep his head and Wallace was never a contender for king.

Bruce's portrait

Since no portrait of Robert the Bruce was made in his lifetime, can we look into the face of the warrior king? The answer is yes – again and again. Numerous reconstructions of his face have been made including versions by Dr Iain Macleod at the Edinburgh Dental Institute, by Mr Brian Hill, the head of Newcastle Dental School, Richard Neave from the University of Manchester and Peter Vanezis from the University of Glasgow.

They are all based on the work of William Scoular, a sculptor who was brought in to draw the skeleton of Bruce. Bruce died in 1329 and was buried in some splendour in Dunfermline Abbey. His ornate tomb was carved in alabaster in France and transported. It was covered in gold leaf and stood in prime position in the abbey. (Fragments of it are in the National Museum of Scotland.) At the time of the Reformation the abbey was badly damaged and the location of the grave was lost.

In 1817 Dunfermline Abbey was due for a rebuild. Workmen found an unusual burial. It was located at the very centre of the ancient cathedral protected by two large stones, a headstone and a much larger stone (6ft in length) into which six iron rings had been fixed. When these stones were removed they found the complete skeletal remains of an individual entirely enclosed in two layers of lead, with what remained of an embroidered linen cloth, with threads of gold, shroud over it. Over the head was a crown made of lead. The tomb was secured.

The following year the grave was reopened for an official examination. Officiating was Sir Henry Jardine, the 'King's Remembrancer'. Observing were several Barons of the Exchequer, Dr Alexander Monro (Professor of Anatomy at Edinburgh University) and other distinguished gentlemen of science.

His heart wasn't in it

Lots of things pointed to this being the body of Bruce: the position of the grave, the gold cloth and the lead crown, but one feature of the skeleton, which might at first seem gruesome, was an important clue. The rib cage on the left side had been sawed through from top to bottom. This was not evidence of some horrific injury, but rather a dying man's wish. Robert the Bruce was buried without his heart. Bruce might be finished but his heart still had places to go.

It had long been Bruce's vow to go on crusade to the holy land to regain the good graces of the Pope, if not the Deity himself. He had run out of time. But if he couldn't go, his heart could.

The heart was encased in a silver casket. The casket was entrusted to Sir James Douglas, who wore it round his neck. The heart was to be taken to the Church of the Holy Sepulchre in Jerusalem and Bruce's vow would be deemed fulfilled. Douglas went off to find a crusade. None were leaving from England or France so he made his way to Spain where it was rumoured that King Alfonso XI was planning to march east. It turned out he was battling the Moorish territory of Grenada, which was right on the Spanish border. In 1330 Douglas and his fellow Scots followed Alfonso into the Battle of Teba.

Pursuing fleeing Muslim cavalry, Douglas is said to have hurled the casket before him, yelling, 'Now pass thou onward before us, as thou wert wont, and I will follow thee or die.' The Muslims turned and the Scots were in retreat. Douglas was trying to withdraw when he saw his companion, Sir William de St Clair of Rosslyn, surrounded by Moorish warriors. Ignoring the odds against him, he moved in with his men to rescue his friend. It was too late. Douglas and most of his men were killed. His body and Bruce's casket were later recovered from the battlefield. Symon Lockhart and William Keith of Galston brought Bruce's heart back to Scotland where it was buried, as the king had requested, in Melrose Abbey. It hadn't got within 2,000 miles of Jerusalem.

'His Majesty's Office of Works'

You would think that the heart would be left in peace, but no. When excavations were taking place in 1996 a lead casket was uncovered. It was whisked off to a secret location at the Gyle near Edinburgh, for fear that Scottish Nationalists might hijack an important Scottish symbol. They carefully drilled a tiny hole and inserted a fibre-optic cable. Imagine the excitement. They were met with a small copper plaque on which they could make out the words 'His Majesty's Office of Works' and the date 1921. This casket, it turned out, contained a smaller one placed in this container for protection when it was unearthed and reburied at that time. In 1921 it was confirmed that the original 9¼in conical container enclosed organic matter and that it could be the heart of Robert the Bruce. There are no records of any other human organs buried there.

In 1996 scientists ran a full battery of modern tests. It was decided that, since there was no chance of recovering DNA, the capsule would not be opened. While no one was prepared to be definite, Mr Richard Wellander, the conservator of artefacts for Historic Scotland, went so far as to say, 'The casket we found was more than likely the one that it is believed Bruce's heart was placed in'. This is as close to sure as you will ever get from an archaeologist.

On the anniversary of the Battle of Bannockburn in 1998, the heart was reburied and a ceremony was held. Apparently, the casket is now protected by several feet of concrete in case those pesky Nationalists get any ideas.

Robert the Bruce had leprosy, or maybe it was just syphilis

But what of the head? As part of the investigation in 1818 an artist, William Scoular, was commissioned to draw the remains. He took the opportunity, while he had the skull of Robert the Bruce in his hands, to create a 3D image. He made a plaster cast of it, which is in the Department of Anatomy at Edinburgh University. Copies were made of the original cast (the department has three) and these turn up in various museums and collections.

There are discrepancies between Jardine's descriptions of the actual skull and the cast, but Jardine was not an anatomist. The skull shows a savage wound, cutting vertically across the left-hand side of his face, denting the skull markedly just above his left eye. A battle scar! For a warrior king noted for being at the front of battle this must have been a badge of honour.

The other tale the skull tells, particularly the teeth and nasal bone structure, is perhaps less kingly. Leprosy? Or not! Among the numerous attempts by artists, sculptors and forensic reconstructionists, some have portrayed a face disfigured by the dread disease and some not. The experts are divided.

Dr Iain MacLeod of the Edinburgh Dental Institute claims that evidence from the skull indicates leprosy and that Bruce was at the centre of a royal cover-up. Lepers would normally be ostracised from society. It would be hard to rule a kingdom from some isolated asylum, so the king's 'problem' was hidden. This does go in the face of evidence that Bruce was meeting people right up to the time of his death and visited Whithorn Abbey shortly before he died.

The one mention of disease, which may have started the whole leprosy rumour, was from an English chronicler. The first reference to the possibility that Bruce might have suffered from leprosy appears in the *Chronicon de Lanercost*, a general history of England and Scotland from 1210 to 1346 which has been attributed to an unknown Franciscan friar at Carlisle. This states that Bruce handed over the command of the army during the Weardale campaign in 1327 'because he had become leprous' when in fact it is documented that Bruce was in Ireland at that time.

Evidence from the skull, given today's techniques, might provide an answer, but the experts all admit that they are working with a Victorian copy. There are some indications of some sort of disease, leprosy perhaps. 'Sporadic syphilis' has also been suggested. For us the most compelling argument is put forward by MacLennan and Kaufman of the Henry Noble History of Dentistry Research Group in 2001:

While Bruce was despised by his English and Scottish enemies, as well as by the Pope, none could find words vile enough to describe him. Of the terms used, and most these days would be considered unprintable, it is curious that he was never referred to as a 'leper', as this was probably the most offensive term available at that time. This alone very strongly suggests that there was probably no contemporary evidence that he suffered from this condition.

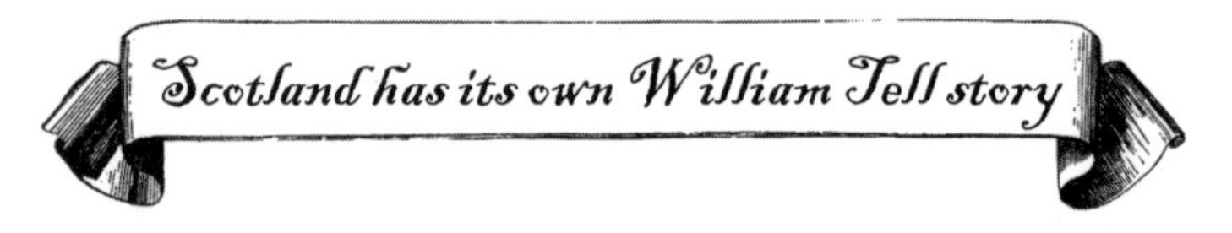

Scotland has its own William Tell story

When Robert the Bruce was established as king he paid a visit to Rothesay Castle on the Isle of Bute, to celebrate the New Year. Naturally he travelled with a considerable retinue. Some of his soldiers fell in with men of the MacKinlay family of the nearby Wester Kames estate. In the spirit of goodwill the young nobles challenged the MacKinlays of Wester Kames to a bit of sport: a friendly shooting match.

As befitted the light-hearted nature of the occasion, there were no regulation targets; it was just a bit of fun. An apple tossed into the sea was the first target. The eldest son of MacKinlay hit it, but so did the King's Man. The next target was a lamb bone; again both men hit their mark.

The elderly MacKinlay was not about to let things lie. He lifted his bow with his son helping the frail old man. He split an apple, then a lamb bone. The score was even.

Old MacKinlay offered an extra challenge. One of his sons stood while an apple was balanced on his head. The frail old man shot, the son stood, and the apple was split. A telling shot. The King's Man pled with his companions, but none would stand for him with an apple on their head. The challenge was unanswered. The MacKinlays won by default.

The King's Men returned to Rothesay, disgruntled. The old man, exhausted, took to his bed, slept and dreamt. He awoke with news from his dream, 'This will be a foul night at Wester Kames!' Guards were posted.

In the town, the men grumbled about their defeat. They feel cheated; they feel that some sort of revenge was due. They headed for Wester Kames. Thanks to the old man's dream, the MacKinlays were ready. The first man rushing in was shot and then the next. At the end of the skirmish, seventeen of the King's Men were dead.

A butler was given a castle

At dawn, Ne'er Day, the first of the year, the King's Spenser (his butler) sensed an opportunity. He chided the waking king about the new year – a gift for unflinching service was surely due!

'What', the King asked, 'should I give you?' The Spenser, armed with knowledge of the night's events, said, 'Anything that will fall into your hands before breakfast, and will cost you nothing.'

Before breakfast the story emerged of the skirmish and the news that the MacKinlays, fearing a king's wrath, had fled, leaving house and lands empty. The estate of Wester Kames had fallen into the king's hands and not cost him a penny! The Spenser took the family name of Spens and occupied Wester Kames for over 400 years.

Being King is not good for your health

In 1371 Bruce's grandson, also Robert, became king. He was the son of Marjory Bruce and Walter Stewart, High Steward of Scotland. He established the Stewart dynasty which would last, officially, 341 years and in the aspirations of the exiled Jacobites, for a few centuries longer.

While Robert II, the first Stewart king, lived to the age of 74 (impressive for the time), later Stewarts did not enjoy such long lives. Their deaths were largely matters of ill luck or ill judgement.

James I, aged 42, died in a sewer. In 1437, trying to escape from a gang of thirty conspirators from among his own noblemen, James crawled down a sewer. Unfortunately he, himself, had ordered that the sewer be blocked a short time before, because he kept losing tennis balls down it. He found himself trapped. He was stabbed and killed.

James II had imported a number of new cannons from Flanders. In 1460 he was besieging Roxburgh Castle when he decided to fire one of the weapons himself. The cannon, called the 'Lion', exploded, fatally injuring the king at the age of 29.

James III was in conflict with his own nobles when he died at, or shortly after, the Battle of Sauchieburn in 1488. There are different versions of the events. He may have died during the battle or may have been intercepted later when he tried to leave the field. Some say he was put off his guard as his assassin was dressed as a priest. Alternatively, a 'great grey horse' presented to him on the eve of the battle by Sir David Lindsay, threw him and

he was killed or murdered where he fell. Whichever way it was, he was dead at the age of 36.

James IV led his men heroically into battle at the disastrous Battle of Flodden and gallantly perished on the field. It is his post-perishing adventures which are less clear. His body was taken to London for an official burial, but the fact that he had been excommunicated by the Church meant that he could not be laid in holy ground. His embalmed body was left, unburied, in an abbey in Surrey. At the Dissolution of the Monasteries, that abbey was heavily damaged and the king disappeared. There were rumours that James IV never left Scotland and the wrong body went south. He has variously been identified as a body found in a well at Hume Castle (which did have the iron chain he habitually wore as a penance), as a skeleton found in Roxburgh Castle, or possibly with a grave site just outside Kelso. Wherever he is he was 40 when he died.

James V was only 30. Shortly after his army suffered a disastrous defeat by the English at the Battle of Solway Moss, he fell ill and retired to Falkland Palace. Some said that it was a nervous collapse brought on by the shame of the defeat. It may just have been a regular fever. It was while he was on his deathbed that his daughter, Mary, was born.

'Mary Queen of Scots had her head chopped off'

Mary had, perhaps, the most publicised death of all the Stewarts. She spent nineteen years as a prisoner, with the possibility of a death sentence hanging over her head all that time. Finally on 7 February 1587 she met the axeman at Fotheringhay Castle. It did not go well. The executioner missed with the first swing, catching her on the back of the head. The second swing cut most of the way through her neck but he had to saw through the remaining sinew with the blade.

He picked up Mary's head by her trademark red hair. Her head rolled across the platform and the axeman was left holding a ginger wig. Mary's hair was grey and close cropped.

Then, to the shock of the onlookers, Mary's body started to move. It transpired that she had brought her lap dog with her to the block wrapped up in her voluminous skirts. The dog refused to leave the body.

The battle of the pot

Most noble families in Scotland have their traditional heartland. It was, however, wise to keep an eye open for the opportunity to get a foothold elsewhere. That might be achieved by marriage or by force, or sometimes both. The Campbell's assault on the Thanedom of Cawdor was certainly audacious, at least geographically.

Others cannot fail to have noticed that in 1498 John the 8th Thane of Cawdor had died, leaving as his sole heir a girl. The girl was not even born at the time of his death. The title, in the hands of a baby, was vulnerable. Whoever held the child held the power. It was the Campbells who made the move.

Directed by Sir Archibald Campbell, a raiding party travelled from Inverary in Argyll all the way to Cawdor Castle, just outside Nairn (over 150 miles on today's roads). They succeeded in kidnapping the baby (the magical tree failing to protect her) and raced back across the hostile country. The Cawdor men were in pursuit.

They eventually surprised the Campbells in a temporary camp. It quickly became apparent that a group of the renegades were taking an undue interest in a large cooking pot upturned in the centre of the camp. Seven sons of Argyll ringed the pot ready to fight to the death to defend it. It was obvious that this was the hiding place of the child. The fight raged and the Campbells were cut down. The pot was eventually overturned to reveal nothing. The baby's minders were well down the road having taken full advantage of the head start provided by the battle for the pot.

The girl, Muriel, grew up in Inverary and at about the age of 12 was married to Sir John Campbell, younger son of Archibald. Things seemed to go well enough and Muriel stayed in Argyll for a further eleven years.

Events took a turn. Around 1520 Sir John's sister, Catherine, had married Lachlan McLean of Duart Castle. It was a good match, but Lachlan was not impressed when Catherine failed to produce children. There was no vital heir. One version of the story claims that Catherine was no whimpering lassie and had tried to kill her husband twice. A solution needed to be found. McLean's solution was to maroon his wife on a rock off the coast (known today as Lady's Rock) and let the incoming tide take its uncaring course. In the morning she was gone.

The grieving McLean duly sent the heartbreaking news of his wife's 'accident' to her father. He responded with an invitation to Inverary to hold a gathering in her honour. McLean was surprised when he entered the hall and found his wife alive and well and sitting by her father's side. She had been rescued from the rock by fishermen and had run straight back to her family.

Dealing with McLean there and then would have created a major incident, but things did not slide for long. On 10 December 1523 he was found, stabbed to death, in Edinburgh. Rumours strongly suggested that John Campbell, Catherine's brother, was responsible.

John decided it might be wise to put himself some distance from the authorities. He gathered his wife, Muriel, and took her north to a land of which she could have no memory but which, as the rightful thaness, she owned.

Of course, those back at Cawdor who had been enjoying the facilities during her twenty-five-year absence were none too happy. Four of Muriel's uncles laid siege to the castle, determined to stop the Campbell upstart. Sir John prevailed, two of the uncles died in the skirmish and the line of the Campbells of Cawdor was established.

The bird man

John Damian de Falcius was an Italian alchemist, a friend of Leonardo Da Vinci. He convinced the king that he could attain the alchemists' dream of turning base metal into gold. When he was mocked for his ongoing failure to produce anything of worth, he announced that he was off to France and that he would fly there from the walls of Stirling Castle.

In 1507 he took his contraption to the walls and launched himself into the air. According to an account by court poet William Dunbar, he didn't quite make it to France but rather plummeted straight to earth. Fortunately he landed right on a dung heap which broke his fall enough for him to escape with only a broken leg.

He claimed that his mistake had been to use chicken feathers. The innate chickenness in the feathers meant that they were naturally attracted to the midden. The king must have been amused as he kept De Falcius on in his service for another six years.

An island experiment

The experiment featured in *New Scientist* magazine, in 2015, was to leave 100 babies on an island with only the minimum resources needed to survive. The point was to see how they would develop language, social structures and a new culture without any influence from the past.

The project was a 'thought experiment'. It was a proposal with experts in a number of fields speculating on the possible outcomes. No babies were harmed in the making of this project.

James IV had no such qualms. He was keen on scientific discovery and supported a bizarre experiment in 1493. A deaf and dumb woman was marooned on Inchkeith Island in the Firth of Forth with two babies. She was to raise the children to see what language they would develop given that they would never have heard a single spoken word.

The theory was that the children would reveal the original language, the language of Eden, the 'Tongue of God'. It turned out to be Hebrew.

Robert Lindsay of Pitscoddie in Fife, an eminent historian, was the author of *The Historie and Chronicles of Scotland*, the first history to be written in Scots instead of the academic language of Latin. He reported that, 'some say that they spoke good Hebrew, for my part I know not but from report'.

The intriguing possibility is that the children could have developed cryptophasia. This scientific term describes the secret language sometimes developed between twins. It is a form of idioglossia (any language used by one or very few people), as I'm sure you guessed.

There are rumours that the island was used during the Second World War. Inchkeith was certainly heavily fortified and a key part of the defence of the Forth. Some theorists murmur about strange unspecified activities related to the atomic bomb and the Manhattan Project. Quite what went on is uncertain.

The Stone of Destiny

This story, as mentioned in the introduction, defies any possibility of setting stories in a neat chronological line. Where does it start? Where does it end? It also emphasises the unavoidable connections between Scotland and Ireland.

The Stone of Destiny? It is a piece of masonry that resonates through Scottish and Irish history. It is well known that Edward I (English king, happy to be known as 'Hammer of the Scots', also tried to hammer the French but that didn't go so well) stole the Stone from Scone Abbey and took it to Westminster Abbey. Every British monarch since has been crowned with this rock beneath their chair.

The symbolism is clear enough. Between 1296 and 1603, when a Scot, James VI and I, was crowned on it, the Stone of Destiny inferred that every King or Queen of England was, by way of the Scottish symbol of coronation, King or Queen of Scotland also. The Stone is currently 'on loan' and is contracted to return to Westminster for any coronation. If Scotland achieves independence it will be interesting to see how this plays out.

That the Stone sat on the Hill of Tara and was the crowning seat of the Ard Righ, the High King, of Ireland is possible. That Fergus MacErc, King of Dalriada, the kingdom that was both in Ireland and in what we now call Scotland, brought the Stone for a coronation ceremony in Argyll is less clear, but plausible. That Kenneth McAlpin, the first King of Scots to also become King of Picts, moved it from Argyll to Scone is pretty much accepted. The first big question is, where did a rock of such awesome power come from in the first place?

The Stone came from the Middle East

To explore this story we have no option but to go back into mythology. The myths (or are they legends?) describe a new people arriving in Ireland (before the Celts). They are called the De Dannan – the children (or grandchildren) of Dana. They bring with them four magical objects: a magic spear, a magic sword, a magic pot and a magic stone. Now what could be magical about them? A more sharply pointed spear than you'd ever seen? Fair enough. But a magic sword? Wouldn't it be magical if you'd never seen one before? A magic pot? A pot that you could put on a fire and boil water in as well as cooking stew in it. Wouldn't it be magical if you'd never seen one before?

Perhaps these stories describe the arrival of metal in Ireland. You can't make a sword out of stone. You can't make a cooking pot out of clay. The arrival of the Bronze Age. And with it comes a 'wee Magic Stane', the *Lia Fail*, the Stone of Destiny, which you can now pay £16.50 and see in Edinburgh Castle.

We can go further back, but it does get vague. The start of the Bronze Age in Ireland coincides with the period in which adventures recorded in the Old Testament took place. In the Old Testament there is a lost tribe, one of the twelve tribes of Israel. The tribe disappears from Middle Eastern history carrying with them a holy stone – a magic stone. This is the stone that Jacob laid his head on to sleep when he saw the vision of a ladder to heaven – Jacob's pillow.

So, a long time before written history, there are two stories. The first one tells of a new people arriving in Ireland called De Dannan, bringing with them a sacred stone, and the other tells of a people disappeared from Middle Eastern history bearing with them a sacred stone. By the way, they were the Tribe of Dan. Maybe that's a clue.

An alternative story is told by Hector Boece in his 'Scotorum Historiae', 1527. A Greek named Gaythius went to Egypt at the time of the Exodus and there married a pharaoh's daughter called Scota. After the biblical destruction of the Egyptian army in the Red Sea, the pair fled. They sailed up the Mediterranean, settling and founding a kingdom in Brigantium, the modern-day Santiago de Compostella in Spain. This was the Kingdom of Scots, followers of Scota. He ruled from a throne consisting of a 'fatal Stone'.

Later a descendant, Simon Breck, brought the stone to Ireland and was crowned king on it. He also brought the name Scot, which then travelled across the North Channel with the Dalriadans. The Simon Breck story is supported by 'Scalacronica', written in 1355 (perhaps that was where Boece got the story from).

If we accept even the possibility that this is a mystical symbol whose roots stretch back to biblical times in the Middle East, the second big question is whether or not the object sitting in Edinburgh Castle is the same piece of stone. The fact that geologists assure us that it is made of Perthshire sandstone, local to Scone from where Edward I stole it, suggests not. The stone is described at various times in its history as being of white marble, at other times of polished black basalt. Sometimes it is said to have an inscription. Jacques Cambray in his 'Monuments Celtiques', from 1805, describes it as having, '*Ni fallat fatum, Scoti quocumque locatum invenient lapidiem, regnasse tenetur ibidem*' which translates as, 'If the Destiny proves true, then the Scots are known to have been Kings wherever men find this stone.' The modern stone is none of these things.

The Stone is real, or at least the story is

So is this potent symbol of Scottish Nationalism a fake? Alex Salmond thinks so; he made that clear in an interview in 2008. The most popular notion is that when Edward I, King of England and Hammer of the Scots, raided Scone Abbey in 1296 the monks had already hidden the real Stone and replaced it with a lump of sandstone from a local burn. This was what Edward took south. As Alex Salmond puts it:

> If you're the abbot of Scone and the strongest and most ruthless king in Christendom is charging toward you in 1296 to steal Scotland's most sacred object and probably put you and half of your cohorts to death, do you do nothing and wait until he arrives or do you hide yourself and the Stone somewhere convenient in the Perthshire hillside? I think the second myself.

If it was stowed away, where did it go? It supposedly did turn up on one occasion. Local tradition has it that around the end of the eighteenth century two farm workers were caught in a torrential downpour on Dunsinane Hill, near Scone. They came across an opening in the ground created by a landslip. The fissure revealed a cavernous passage which they explored, and found a stone-built chamber. A staircase in one corner was blocked by rubble. In the centre of the chamber was a slab of stone resting on four stone legs. The Stone! Apparently the two lads didn't draw that conclusion and didn't realise the importance of their find. The story only emerged later. When people went searching for the opening, it, of course, could not be found.

The only compelling reason for thinking that Edward had the real thing was put forward by Ian Hamilton: 'Had it been a substitute for Edward to carry off it would have been produced when the king (Robert the Bruce) regained his kingdom. It wasn't.' It is likely that the Scots would not have missed the chance to stick two fingers up at the English king if they had the opportunity.

'A Stane wi' a ring!'

The story can once again go backward or forward. The next most popular chance to switch stones was in 1951. The Stone was stolen from Westminster Abbey. Ian Hamilton and fellow students Gavin Vernon, Alan Stuart and Kay Matheson broke into the abbey on Christmas Eve intent on theft. Things did not go smoothly; in fact it was something of a farce which included the Stone being dropped and breaking into two pieces (which, Ian Hamilton noted, made it easier to carry). Nonetheless they got away with their prize. Despite a huge police mobilisation, including road blocks on the Border, they got it back to Scotland.

'Not,' said Ian Hamilton, in an interview in the *Telegraph*, 'that it was stealing. It was a liberation. A returning of a venerable relic to its rightful ownership.' Scottish Nationalism was at an all-time low (with the SNP on 0.7 per cent of the vote). 'I wanted to waken the Scots up, that was all,' said Hamilton.

The Stone was eventually returned. It was left symbolically in Arbroath Abbey where the Declaration of Arbroath was signed. But was it the same stone that had been taken from Westminster? There are doubts. The Stone was taken to a stonemason, Bertie Gray, to assess the damage and it is thought that he made several copies. One of these may have been what was returned.

'There's no question that Bertie Gray made copies,' said Alex Salmond. 'It's like the Loch Ness monster, it's certainly a puzzle and a mystery which is best not definitively answered.'

Perhaps a verse from Johnny McEvoy's song 'The Wee Magic Stane' is apt:

> So if ever ye come on a Stane wi' a ring
> Just sit yersel' doon and proclaim yersel' King.
> For there's nane wid be able tae challenge yer claim
> That ye'd crowned yersel' King on the Destiny Stane.

It has also been suggested that the real Stone never left Ireland or that it is still in Argyll, and that the one in Scone wasn't genuine in the first place. Red sandstone, black basalt, white marble? What does it really matter? Surely it is the symbol, the story, that is important. 'I felt I was holding Scotland's soul when I touched it,' said Ian Hamilton.

If the symbol is important then its location is important too. In 1996 British Prime Minister John Major conceded. The *Lia Fail*, the Stane o' Scone, the Stone of Destiny, the Wee Magic Stane, crossed the border in a Land Rover. On St Andrew's Day it was unveiled alongside the Honours of Scotland in Edinburgh Castle. Since then Scottish Nationalism has gone from strength to strength. In 2015 they took all but three Scottish seats in the national election. Maybe the Stone does have power after all.

The Auld Alliance

The Auld Alliance was a treaty between Scotland and France agreeing that should either country be attacked by England the other would invade English territory. The treaty was signed by John Balliol, who was briefly King of Scotland before Robert the Bruce and Philip IV of France.

The treaty was renewed repeatedly. The final review was in 1588 when Mary Queen of Scots was betrothed to the French heir to the throne (they were both children – Francis, who was to be Francis II, died long before the marriage).

While there were promises and a few pale efforts of support for Scotland, France seems to have done better out of the deal. As many as 15,000 Scottish troops served in France against Henry V and it was a joint Scottish and French force which won the Battle of Bauge in 1421.

In 1429 Joan of Arc marched to 'Scots Wha Hae'

Legend has it that the besieged citizens of the city of Orleans took heart when they heard the pipes approaching and knew there was a significant Scottish contingent (under John Stewart of Darnley) in the rescue force. Joan is said to have entered the city to the Scots tune 'Hey, Tuttie Tattie', a tune which Robert Burns used (much later, of course) for his song 'Scots Wha Hae'. Recent attempts to celebrate the Scots' involvement in the campaign are ongoing.

The Scots Guard were loyal bodyguards to the French monarchy

The Scots Guard, not to be confused with the British regiment of the same name, was formed in 1418 and bolstered by James II in 1450. The Scots unit continued (through different administrative changes) until finally being officially disbanded in 1830.

Given the long history of Scottish soldiering in France (it is likely that Scots fought for Charlemagne before AD 800) it is not surprising that many 'sojers' married and settled in France. Many got lands and titles. But it was not just a military matter. Scots studied at French universities, influencing Scots law; Scots living in France could automatically claim French citizenship from 1513. This was not rescinded until 1903.

Scotland was favoured in trade too, especially in one vital commodity which we'll come to shortly.

The breakdown in the alliance comes down to religion. When the Reformation saw Scotland become a firmly Protestant country (officially) the connection with France, which was still Catholic, couldn't be sustained. It was widely assumed that the Treaty of Leith (or Treaty of Edinburgh) annulled the Auld Alliance. This treaty followed the Siege of Leith, when a contingent of French soldiers was surrounded by English troops. Historian Dr Siobhan Talbot, in 2011, published the results of a four-year study into all the relevant paperwork. She came to the conclusion that there is nothing in that treaty or any other document which actually rescinds the Auld Alliance.

This revelation means that the alliance is actually the oldest enduring treaty in the world, lasting from 1295 to now, 720 years as we write. The sweet thing in the banter with the 'Auld Enemy' is that this now trumps England's claim to having the oldest enduring alliance. England signed a treaty with Portugal as recently as 1373, which was claiming the record.

Now Scotland can demonstrate that we win by seventy-eight years. Score to us, we think.

What you drink is a taste of your loyalty

Claret is the true drink of Scotland. The relationship between Scotland and France, and the relationship between England and Portugal, influenced our favoured beverages.

Scots merchants had access to the best of claret. English dealers only got second best. Port was available to the English. It was the English drink. Claret is the Scottish drink!

If you were to toast 'The King O'er the Watter' in deference to the lost Jacobite kings, the correct liquid would be claret. Whisky was something for the lower classes.

The first licence to distil whisky

While we're on the subject of drink, what about whisky? When Sir Thomas Phillips, a former English soldier, was in the process of developing the town of Coleraine in the north of Ireland, he obtained permission to fell timber, to hold markets and, in 1608, to distil whisky. This licence, granted by James VI and I, gave him leave 'to make, drawe, and distil such and soe great quantities of aquavite, usquabagh and aqua composita, as he or his assignes shall thinke fitt'.

The area which was covered was County Coleraine and 'the Route'. The Route is the area of County Antrim which was planted with Scots by Randal MacDonnell. The Bushmills Distillery claims that licence as part of its heritage and calls itself the oldest whiskey in the world. While Bushmills is certainly within the Route, it was not at any point part of Sir Thomas Phillips' domain (though he did rent the nearby town of Portrush for one hogshead of claret per annum). If he was making whisky it was likely to be in his base at Coleraine.

Of course, the first licence does not mean the first whisky. The first suggestion of distilled spirit goes back to the Babylonians over 1,000 years before Christ. Certainly the ancient Greeks had the art. The date of the first Scottish dram is unknown, but when it comes to written records the Irish have the lead. The first Irish record is from 1405 when a chieftain is said to have died from a surfeit of aqua vitae while having a very merry Christmas. The first Scottish mention is not until 1494 in the Exchequer Rolls.

In any case, at the time of Sir Thomas' licence, the favoured drink in Scotland amongst people of class was claret.

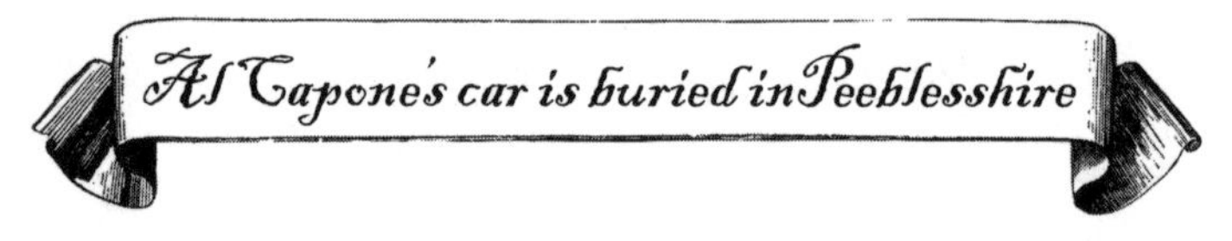

An estate near Innerleithen was once owned by William Crockett Miller-Thomson, who was one of the many Scots involved in supplying whisky to America during prohibition. Miller-Thomson became friends with Al Capone and bought his car from him. He had it shipped back to Scotland. It is supposedly still hidden in the grounds.

A *Fortune* magazine article from the 1930s reported that in 1913 Scotch (and a little Irish) sales were 1.5 million gallons compared to 135 million gallons of American whiskey. By the end of thirteen years of prohibition Scotch consumption had soared and had become firmly established as an American favourite (over 160 million gallons in 2013 according to the Scotch Whisky Association).

While perhaps not breaking the law, strictly speaking, many major Scottish distillers were knowingly supplying large quantities of their product to infamous gangsters like Capone, 'Legs' Diamond and Bugsy Siegel.

The technique was simple enough. The whisky was transported to the Bahamas, then a British colony. Imports of Scotch to the island went from under 1,000 to over 350,000 gallons in three years. The product changed hands and was transferred into vessels which then patrolled just outside US coastal waters. Fast speedboats ferried it ashore. It took the US Coast Guard years before it managed to obtain new boats fast enough to challenge the gangsters.

Such familiar names as Dewars, Chivas, Johnny Walker and the Distillers Company were among those involved in the enterprise. Charles Maclean, the author of *Scotch Whisky: A Liquid History*, said, 'Prohibition was the best thing that ever happened to Scotch'.

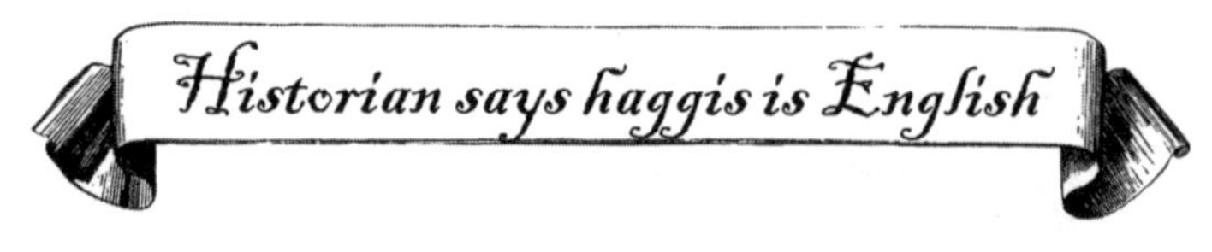

In a shock-horror announcement in 2009 promoted by both ITV and the BBC, historian Catherine Brown revealed that haggis is in fact an English invention. In support of this she cites a recipe book called the *English Hus Wyf* published in 1615 by Gervaise Markham. While this may be the first published recipe, there is a reference to 'haggeis' in the *Flyting of Dunbar and Kennedy* from before 1520. Flyting is a form of poetic sparring in which the combatants fling verse at each other. But then again there is a reference to 'hagese' in the book *Liber Coure Cocorum* from Lancashire in 1430.

By the way, in 2008 Professor Ferenc Szasz of the University of New Mexico said modern rap music, which was developed by African-American youths in New York's Bronx borough, descended from the Scottish practice of flyting. This had been communicated to the slave population through the involvement of Scots in the American South plantations – seriously!

It has been claimed that haggis was known to the Ancient Romans or maybe the Ancient Greeks. Some say it was brought here by the Vikings, some that it has all the hallmarks of a French peasant dish.

The thing is that Scots know all these things and, frankly, don't care. We are the only country to venerate the haggis in our national literature, through Robert Burns. We are the only country to feature it in one of our most important annual celebrations, the Burns Supper. We are the only nation to turn it into a sport! Haggis hurling consists of hurling a haggis down a park while standing on a whisky barrel. (The world record at the time of writing is 214ft 9in and is held by Lorne Coltart of Blair Atholl.) We are the only people to eat it deep-fried in batter with chips. We kinna think that we own the haggis.

When it comes down to it, inventing haggis is not a huge leap. If you have a freshly gralloched sheep you have a pile of (potentially tasty) mushy bits – liver, heart, kidney and lungs – that you don't want to waste. You also have on hand a handy container, namely the sheep's stomach. Now you have an easily transported package that is also an effective cooking receptacle – the first 'boil-in-a-bag' meal. Just add hot water. The fact that you also fling in a 'handfu' o' porridge' gives us a nod in a Scottish direction.

Wild haggis

Every Scot knows that haggises (haggi is definitely wrong – it would have to be haggUS before it could become haggI – yes, we are old enough to have done Latin at school) are wild creatures that live in the highlands and have one pair of legs shorter than the other to facilitate running around mountains. This makes them easy to catch if you approach from the opposite direction as they can't turn around. Every Scot also thinks that it is hilarious that 30 per cent of Americans, in a recent poll, believe this to be true.

By the way, haggis has been banned in the United States – they do not consider it fit for human consumption. Or at least they consider the lung it contains as unfit.

Haggis should be bought from a local family butcher (though some of the commercially produced stuff is not bad). Each will have their own recipe which they will defend to the death. There are correct ways to eat the beast – that is with tatties (potatoes) and neeps (turnip or, more correctly, swede).

A photograph we came across on a BBC website was horribly wrong – the tatties 'werenae champit' (mashed). And there was some green stuff on the plate!

Haggis can properly be eaten in batter, but only from a bona fide Scottish chippie (preferably run by an Italian family). That said, recent attempts by chefs to use haggis in a wide variety of experimental dishes are to be applauded.

'It Will Pass With a Lass'

The sixteenth century has been described as the beginning of the modern world. It began with the scientific curiosity of James IV and ended with the burning of witches by James VI. In between was the tangled and tragic life of Mary, Queen of Scots.

James V got it wrong, yet got it right

When James V said 'It came with a lass, and it will pass with a lass' on the birth of his daughter, Mary, he was referring to the Stewart dynasty. The lass that started it was Marjory Bruce, daughter of Robert the Bruce, who married Walter Stewart, giving the family the right to the throne. He was predicting that his daughter's reign would see the end of it. He was spectacularly wrong. Mary's son (who she barely knew as he grew up) was to become James I of England. Stewarts would be monarchs of both Scotland and England for another 165 years (with a slight interruption).

By the way, the 'Stewarts' were now 'Stuarts'. The change of spelling was made by Mary so as to make it easier for the French to pronounce correctly.

James V was also right. The Stuart reign did indeed end with a lass: Queen Anne, daughter of James VII. She was pregnant seventeen times, but died without any living children. Anne's brother, James Frances, was excluded as he was a Catholic. This led, through a complicated calculation, to the arrival of the German House of Hanover and a long succession of Georges.

Mary Queen of Ghosts

Mary, Queen of Scots' life was certainly strange. Queen at the age of six days, she was brought up in the French court and was engaged to a French prince (who died). She arrived in Scotland to find herself regarded as the enemy by the English and quite a few Scots. Her husband, Darnley, murdered her friend, Rizzio. Darnley was then murdered. Mary dashed off with one of her husband's murderers, Bothwell. She was imprisoned on an island in Loch Leven. She escaped and fled to England where she was kept a prisoner for nineteen years before her strange and gruesome death.

Since then she has been a very busy lady. Ghosts are often said to be restless spirits and Mary's is more restless than most. During her travails in Scotland and her detention in England she stayed in many castles and grand houses. Apparently, at many of them she is still there.

Stirling Castle was a familiar place to her; she allegedly remains there in a pink dress (the one in the green dress is a maid who rescued her mistress when her bed caught fire). Her ghost lingers on the isle in Loch Leven. At Borthwick Castle, where she stayed with Bothwell, a spectral boy appears and, yes, it's Mary again wearing the disguise in which she escaped the castle. Bothwell connects her to Hermitage Castle, which she haunts – even though she never stayed there! She appears, headlessly, at Craignethan, near Lanark. She may, or may not be, the white lady who appears on the stairs at Craigmillar Castle. This Mary only appears when it's raining heavily outside!

During her English adventures she was kept at Bolton Castle, where she still wanders around the courtyard. At Nappa Hall in Yorkshire she wears a black gown. She also walks through walls in the Earl's Manor Lodge in Sheffield.

Fotheringay, the place of her execution, is a likely candidate for a ghost, but it was destroyed in the seventeenth century. Enterprisingly, when stones and timber from the castle were used to build a hotel nearby, Mary's ghost went with them.

Mary, Queen of Ghosts!

Free murder

In 1551 English Crown Officers declared:

> All Englishmen and Scottishmen, after this proclamation made, are and shall be free to rob, burn, spoil, slay, murder and destroy all and every such persons, their bodies, buildings, goods and cattle as do remain or shall inhabit upon any part of the said Debateable Land without any redress to be made for the same.

The Scottish king had no objection.

The said 'Debatable Land' was the area bounded by the River Esk and the River Liddel on the one side and the River Sark on the other. The whole of the area around the Scotland/ England border was lawless, but neither country had any semblance of authority in this region.

The Border Clans had their own law. Their occupation was 'reiving': stealing – cows mainly, but whatever came to hand. They were happy to raid north or south from their strongholds.

By the way, the word 'blackmail' came from the Border reivers. It referred to the protection rackets they ran – 'pay up or lose yer coos or yer heid'.

Armstrongs, Kerrs, Elliots, Grahams, Humes and Bothwells had little regard for either king. The Armstrongs were one of the strongest families: they claimed to be able to muster 3,000 armed men. In 1530 King James V took action. He went hunting.

A Borders Hunting Party

James set off, with an entourage suitable for his purpose, to Ettrick Forest (pretty much Selkirkshire today).

By the way, a 'forest' denotes a hunting area; trees are in no way implied. Much of the Highlands were given over to 'deer forests', when often there was not a tree in sight.

The king camped at Caerlanrig on the River Teviot. He issued an invitation to the Border gentlemen to join him there. Here was an opportunity for reconciliation. If they were prepared to swear their loyalty all would be forgiven.

Young Johnnie Armstrong of Gilnockie, son of the Armstong chief, was sufficiently reassured about his safety that he set out from Langholm Castle with a party of fellow Borderers. The numbers vary from different accounts: there may have been as many as fifty of them, some accounts mention twenty-four; a couple of dozen seems a reasonable number to us.

For such a prestigious occasion the men turned out in their finest clothes and the likes of Johnny Armstrong were not short of cash. The sight of the well-dressed, handsome, confident young man was only a further annoyance. The king was later to say that the reason Johnny Armstrong was killed was because he was better dressed than himself and that was a show of disrespect.

Armstrong's men were intercepted by horsemen before they reached Caerlanrig; it was clear that James hadn't come loaded for deer. Confronted by the king, it was pretty clear that forgiveness was not on the agenda. Johnny claimed that he had only ever raided the south, only robbed the English, to which a modern Glaswegian might reply, 'Aye, right!' (Much has been made of the grammatical incorrectness of the double negative, but 'Aye, right!' is a rare expression that proves that two positives can make a negative.)

The Borderer did not plead for mercy but rather tried to bribe the king. He could afford it. Armstrong is supposed to have said, 'I am but a fool to seek grace at a graceless face, but had I known you would have taken me this day, I would have lived in the Borders despite King Harry (Henry VIII) and you both.'

James hanged the entire Borders party. The game book for the outing might have read, 'Deer –nil, Borderers – twenty-four'.

By the way, the site of the mass grave where they were deposited was unknown until the 1980s when a farmer tilling opposite Caerlanrig church unearthed a large stone with marks on it. Subsequent explorations by dowsers and by archaeologists agreed that there are bodies beneath the spot.

James VI did away with the Scottish Borders

When James VI of Scotland became James I of England he envisaged a united nation. The Border was redundant and the Borderers an embarrassment. They were a threat to travel and to commerce between two parts of his domain. Since that domain stretched from Land's End to John O'Groats, the Borders were halfway down. He rechristened them the 'Middle Shires'.

James commenced a thorough campaign, destroying strongholds and executing or displacing many of the reivers and their families.

Although not part of the official plantation, many of those displaced ended up in Ulster. A range of Borders names are common in Northern Ireland today.

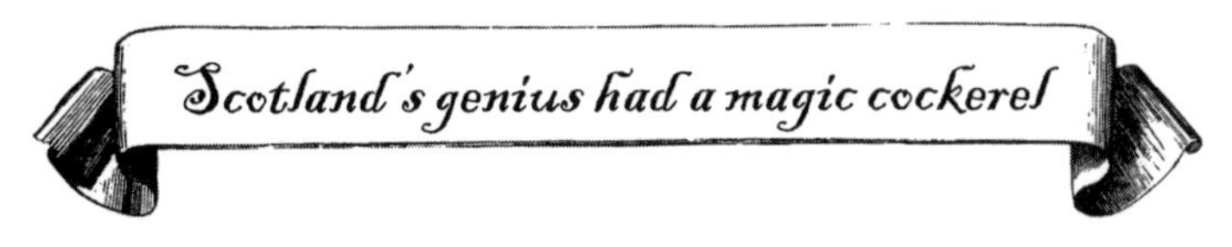

At school we both hated John Napier, although we had never heard his name. He was the inventor of schoolchild torture in the form of logarithms and the decimal notation for complex equations. While we were totally bewildered trying to make sense of these dancing numbers they were, for mathematicians and for all the other disciplines that depend on hard sums, a godsend. He went further with the invention of Napier's Bones, an early calculator, and then followed this with the creation of rabdology, literally 'rod calculation'. The Babbbage Institute has reproduced his work in their history of computing.

His work was revolutionary. His discoveries were right up there with the likes of Galileo and Newton. Scottish intellectual David Hume described him as 'the person to whom the title of great man is more justly due than to any other whom this country has produced'.

At a time in history when any hint of witchcraft was highly dangerous, he was widely rumoured to be a warlock and sorcerer. Dangerous too was being caught on the wrong side of the Protestant/Catholic divide when the followers of Queen Mary were trying to promote the old religion and the forces of the Reformation were trying to stamp it out. At 17 he was forced to study abroad, having left St Andrews University prematurely after his friendship with a Catholic student brought him under suspicion.

He was later to establish his Protestant credentials by publishing an investigation of the biblical prophecies of Armageddon. His conclusion was that the Pope was in fact the Anti-Christ. He went on to write a series of religious tracts which were translated into several languages and sold well across Protestant Europe.

He returned to Edinburgh in 1571 to find his father imprisoned in Edinburgh Castle by the Queen's party, while the family home at Merchiston was occupied by the forces of the regent. The following year Merchiston was bombarded by the guns of Edinburgh Castle.

Retiring from Edinburgh, he built a new house for himself and his young wife at Gartness on the banks of the River Endrick. Elizabeth Stirling left him one child before her premature death. His second wife, Agnes Chisholm from Perthshire, gave him five sons and daughters.

The rural retreat gave him peace to get on with his studies, but Napier's genius was interpreted as foul black wizardry. Rumours of witchcraft grew. He did very little to discourage it; dressed in a long black cloak, with a long black beard, he looked the part. Added to this he openly kept a 'familiar' in the form of a large black cockerel. There is a story that when it was suspected that one of the servants was stealing from the household, he gathered the staff together and bade them stroke the rooster. The bird would identify the guilty party by crowing. He left them to perform the ritual in private. The cock did not crow but Napier quickly identified the thief. He had taken the precaution of spreading soot on the bird's back. The one with clean hands, the one who had not dared stroke the bird, was judged guilty.

He went on to turn his agile mind to agricultural improvement and to military technology. When the Spanish invasion threat was at its height he published *Secrete Inventiones* in which he outlined plans for a giant mirror to burn enemy ships by focusing the sun's rays on them, a man-powered tank, a submarine, and a form of artillery which could clear a field of anything standing over a foot high. None of the ideas ever went into production – he was way ahead of his time.

John Napier is remembered at Napier University in Edinburgh. The university's buildings include Merchiston Tower where he was born.

Witch hunting

The Scots embraced the sport of witch hunting, burning, hanging and drowning more wholeheartedly than other parts of the British Isles. This may have a lot to do with King James VI. He became something of an expert on the subject of witchcraft, even writing a book on the subject, *Daemonologie*.

The whole craze really kicked off with the North Berwick Witch Trials in 1591.

The witches of North Berwick tried to drown the King in the Firth of Forth

James was in Denmark, picking up his wife, Ann of Denmark. His return to Scotland was postponed repeatedly by bad weather. Eventually they made the crossing only to be assaulted by a violent storm while within sight of home. They only just made it to harbour.

It turned out that a party of witches had gathered in North Berwick. They had a cat which they 'christened' James and passed back and forth over the flames of a fire. They set sail to intercept the king's ship in sieves. They were able to listen to conversations on board the vessel. They threw the cat into the sea, conjuring the tempest which nearly sank the king.

Now this might seem strange, but the fact is that this was presented as evidence in a Scottish court. James paid close attention to the whole affair. He did, after all, know a thing or two about the subject. He had during his recent visit to Denmark spent time with renowned witchcraft expert Peter Munk. Thoughts of the things he had learned were fresh in his mind when that storm hit.

Gillis Duncan, a serving girl from Tranent, who had a small reputation as a healer with some knowledge of herbs, was arrested. Under extreme torture she started naming names: Agnes Sampson, an old lady from Haddington; Agnes Tompson of Edinburgh; Dr Fian, a schoolteacher from Saltpans; George Mott's wife; Robert Grierson, a skipper; and Jannet Blandilands. There was more torture and more names emerged. By the end of a two-year trial over seventy people had been implicated.

The guilty one was acquitted

Strangely, the one suspect who might have been guilty of conspiring against the king was the one who got away: Francis Stewart, 5th Earl of Bothwell. He had already been found guilty of conspiring to seize James (his first cousin) at Holyroodhouse two years earlier.

Bothwell was accused of bursting open the door to North Berwick church using a 'Hand of Glory'. A 'Hand of Glory' is the hand cut from a hanged man on the gibbet. When the fingers are lit, like a five-pointed candle, it becomes a powerful magical weapon. Witnesses then described the demonic service conducted by a masked man – Bothwell. Bothwell was arrested but escaped from prison and was declared an outlaw.

In 1593 he forced his way into the royal bedchamber and somehow got the king to grant him a full pardon. His forfeited lands and titles were returned. A trial, regarded by many as a farce, saw him acquitted of the witchcraft charges.

He was later exiled and died in Naples, but he certainly did fare a lot better than many of the others in the trials. Dozens were executed by garrotting, hanging and burning.

The Survey of Scottish Witchcraft has identified 3,837 people accused of witchcraft in Scotland, but admits that this may not be complete. It is unclear how many were executed. In some cases, notably the North Berwick one, torture was used until a confession was forthcoming. There are cases where a conviction was secured on the grounds that the accused did not confess. It was argued that they could only have withstood the pain by means of magic: Catch 22.

The last witches

The last witch burned in Scotland

In 1727 Janet Horne, an elderly woman from Dornoch in Sutherland, was accused by her neighbours of witchcraft. It was said she could turn her daughter into a pony and ride her around in the night. Deformities of the poor girl's hands and feet were cited as evidence.

Janet and her daughter were tried and found guilty. The daughter escaped but the mother was smothered with tar, carried through the town on a barrel and burned to death. Eight years later the law regarding witches was changed.

A small stone monument stands at the spot of her execution. The stone carries the incorrect date 1722.

The last time a Scot was tried under the Witchcraft Act was in 1944

Helen Duncan from Callender was tried at the Old Bailey under the Witchcraft Act of 1735 in 1944. Helen was a well-known fortune teller, astrologer and spiritualist. Arrested following a séance, she was accused of pretending 'to exercise or use human conjuration that through the agency of Helen Duncan spirits of deceased persons should appear to be present'.

She was not, as reported in the press, tried as a witch. In fact the 1735 Act intended to stamp out belief in witchcraft among the general population. Its introduction meant that from 1735 onwards an individual could no longer be tried as a witch in England or Scotland. However, they could be fined or imprisoned for purporting to have the powers of a witch.

During the case she was asked if she could demonstrate her powers from the dock: effectively conduct a séance in the courtroom. She declined. Helen was convicted and sentenced to nine months in prison.

The Fife adventure

James VI was keen on the idea of plantation; simply move a substantial number of people who are sympathetic to you into an area and let them do the job of subduing the natives. This was cheaper than sending in an army and you can, in due course, tax the new settlers.

It is well-known that James supported the plantation of Ulster and Virginia, but he also attempted to plant Bermuda and, bizarrely, the Isle of Lewis.

In 1597 Torquil Dubh MacLeod had failed to comply with the Act of Estates, which compelled everyone who claimed to own land in the Highlands and Islands to produce documentary proof. This left the Isle of Lewis technically ownerless. In 1598 the land was granted to a consortium of businessmen from Fife headed by the Duke of Lennox. They were given seven years rent free to allow them time to establish themselves.

The object was to civilise the natives who were described as guilty of 'the grossest impiety and the most atrocious barbarities'. Commissioners were given authority to punish by 'military execution' anyone who opposed the occupation – either openly or tacitly.

In 1599 the first expedition arrived with a few gentlemen and the builders and tradesmen needed to start construction of the new settlement. They also brought over 500 hired soldiers.

One of the leading Fifers, James Leirmonth, was captured by Murdoch MacLeod when he tried to sail back to Fife and held prisoner until a rich ransom was agreed. Leirmonth, however, died from illness contracted during his captivity and the ransom was never paid. Murdoch's brother, Neil, was persuaded by the settlers to hand over his brother. Murdoch was duly executed in St Andrews.

Peace did not last long. The settlement was attacked, the fort burned and many were killed. The MacLeods demanded that the Fifers leave, never to return, and that the islanders should receive a pardon for all crimes. Hostages were held.

It was not until the summer of 1605 that the Fifers returned. They were armed with:

> Commissions of fire and sword … to search, seek, take and apprehend the aforesaid persons, rebels and fugitives … and execute them to the death; and, if need be, to raise fire and sword and to burn their houses and slay them in case they make opposition or resistance in the taking and apprehending.

They also had a few of the king's ships and an armada of commandeered vessels. They re-established the settlement, but Neil MacLeod did not go away. Under continuing relentless harrying from the natives the whole project slowly crumbled.

By the way, Fife is properly referred to as the 'Kingdom of Fife' (not 'County Fife' as Johnny Cash described it; apparently that's where his ancestors came from). The origins of this appellation are somewhat obscure, as is the question 'Who is the King of Fife?'

Waiting in the wings was Kenneth MacKenzie of Kintail who had long had his eye on Lewis. He stepped in and bought the commission for Lewis from the remaining Fife businessmen for a sum of money and an iron mine in Letterewe. In 1609 MacKenzie, with 700 men, ruthlessly cleared Lewis of opposition, succeeding where the Fifers had failed.

Neil Macleod retreated to the tiny island of Berrisay with a group of loyal men. For three years they held out on this impregnable rock. When his patience ran out Roderick MacKenzie, Kenneth's brother, came up with a dastardly scheme. He rounded up every woman and child related in any way to any of the men on MacLeod's island. He ferried them to a rock that could clearly be seen from Berrisay and announced that there they would stay until the incoming tide swept them away, unless MacLeod gave up his stronghold. Neil immediately complied, but got away himself to his kinsman, Roderick MacLeod of Harris. Roderick persuaded him to go to Edinburgh to seek a pardon. On entering the city Neil was seized and promptly executed. The last of the Highland rebels was gone.

'A Stony Couch for a Deep Feather Bed'

The seventeenth century started with 'Union of the Crowns' – Scotland, England and Ireland were united under a single monarch. A chance for unity, peace and prosperity, perhaps? Unfortunately not! The century was to see the English Civil War spilling over into Scotland and Ireland, the beheading of a Stuart king, the deposing of another Stuart king and Williamite campaigns in Scotland and Ireland.

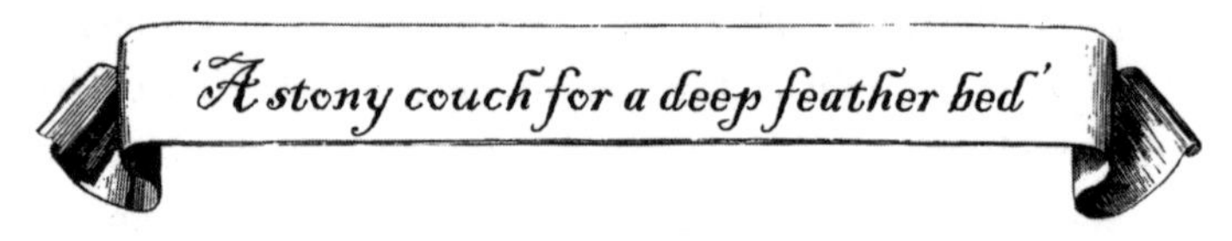

In 1603 James VI of Scotland became James I of England. His great-grandmother, Margaret Tudor, was Henry VIII's oldest sister. It made him the closest candidate in the royal line. He ruled the three kingdoms (he was King of Ireland too) for twenty-two years. Opinions were mixed: David Hume wrote that 'many virtues ... it must be owned, he was possessed of, but no one of them pure, or free from the contagion of the neighbouring vices,' whilst Henry IV of France called James 'the wisest fool in Christendom'.

By and large he maintained peace, ending the long-running conflict with the Spanish, and kept taxes reasonable. Despite conspiracies against him, notably the Gunpowder Plot, he avoided large-scale executions of Catholics by his predecessor, Queen Elizabeth, and of Protestants by Queen Mary before her.

James left Edinburgh, promising to return every three years. He only managed to make it to Scotland once in twenty-two years. He claimed that he ruled Scotland 'with the stroke of a pen'. Despite the huge sums spent by Elizabeth on war against the Spanish and the Irish, James enjoyed the comforts of London. He said he was 'swapping a stony couch for a deep feather bed'.

> By the way, there is considerable conjecture that he was not always alone in the feather bed. He had a succession of young men as 'favourites'. Of one of these he said, 'You may be sure that I love the Earl of Buckingham more than anyone else'. On the other hand he did describe sodomy as among those 'horrible crimes which ye are bound in conscience never to forgive'. The case is 'not proven'.

Scots in Ulster

Despite the failure of the Isle of Lewis scheme, James pursued his idea of 'plantation' as a way of calming troubled lands. The plantation of Ulster was his way of dealing with the most wild, unruly and most Gaelic part of Ireland, the north.

The Ulster Plantation came about through a number of different projects. One of them started almost by accident as a result of a struggle between the MacDonalds and the Campbells in Kintail.

The MacDonalds had lost land in Kintail to their ancient enemies the Campbells. The Campbells, seeking to ensure their hold on the land and to make a profit from it, imported numbers of Protestant Lowland Scots farmers from Renfrewshire and Ayrshire. When the MacDonalds took back the land they were burdened by this population of Lowlanders that they had no use for. How to get rid of them?

Kinsman Randal Arranach MacDonnell residing in Dunluce Castle in County Antrim in Northern Ireland said, 'I'll have them. So long as they've got their own cows.' So began the MacDonnell plantation of County Antrim in 1607 three years before King James IV and I's 'official' plantation got underway.

The MacDonnells of Dunluce in Northern Ireland are often described as Scottish invaders, but they were no strangers. Their recent ancestry was very closely entwined with Ulster families.

To give the background: the MacDonalds of Islay, part of the great MacDonald Clan, came to take over the area of Ulster which today represents most of County Antrim. Islay, remember, is clearly visible from Ireland and vice versa, a short hop in a Highland Galley.

Their first claim to the area was through marriage, John Mor MacDonald (Big John) and Margaret Bisset, giving them title to the Glens area, but it was a couple of generations later before the MacDonalds made a substantial move. Sorley Boy MacDonnell became the occupier of Dunluce Castle and the master of a substantial territory. Sorley Boy's granny was from Ulster, so was his great-granny and his great-great-granny and so on. In fact six out of seven of his immediate ancestors had married Ulster women. He was related to all the great families of the province: O'Neills, O'Cahans, Bissets, Savages and O'Donnells.

300,000 acres of Ulster stayed in the hands of a Scottish Catholic

While the project of the plantation of Ulster was supposed to have replaced the native population with Lowland Scottish and English Protestants, 300,000 acres remained in the hands of a Scottish Highland Roman Catholic.

Randal Arranach MacDonald had maintained his links across the North Channel. The name 'Arranach' indicates that he grew up on the Isle of Arran following a custom of fostering out children to strengthen family ties. He had an entirely Highland upbringing.

During the Nine Years' War he had started out against the forces of Queen Elizabeth, but had listened to the wind and at the opportune moment switched sides and declared himself a loyal English servant.

The end of that war coincided with the death of Elizabeth and the accession of James I; indeed, when Hugh O'Neill, the Ulster commander, surrendered to a portrait of Queen Elizabeth nobody mentioned that she had been dead for three days.

James was looking for a different solution. He hated war. Not that he was a nice man, but war cost money, lots of it. Coming to London from his impoverished position in Scotland he found the coffers empty and property mortgaged – all to finance war in Ireland.

His alternative solution for Ulster, the wildest and most Gaelic part of Ireland, was plantation. There were different schemes and exceptions, but largely land was taken from the Irish clans and given to English and Scottish gentlemen in portions of up to 3,000 acres. They were then expected to import tradesmen, famers and labourers to work that land and to build a new infrastructure.

The MacDonnell clan were sitting on most of County Antrim. His opposite number, chief of the O'Cahan clan, on the other side of the River Bann, was arrested and sent to the Tower of London where he spent over twenty years without a single charge being brought against him. He was simply got rid of.

Thanks to his Lowlanders from Kintail, Randal MacDonnell could claim that there was no need to take his land away as he was already planting it with the appropriate sort. He got away with it. His English neighbours repeatedly accused him of remaining a Catholic, harbouring priests. Each time the king, while noting that these were grievous offences, pardoned him. Some say that this was due to liaisons the two men had in Scotland in earlier years. The MacDonnells were the only Ulster clan to retain their lands and position. The family continue to be Earls of Antrim to this day.

There is no Ulster–English tradition

Many in Ulster are intensely proud of their Scottish origins. Ulster Scots heritage is widely celebrated, but there is never a whisper about Ulster English!

MacDonnell's plantation in Antrim was Scottish, as was the Hamilton and Montgomery (both of whom were from Ayrshire) plantation in County Down, however overall 40 per cent of the planters were from England. County Londonderry was planted from London, hence the name. It is our experience that many folk in Ulster will flatly refuse to contemplate that their ancestors were anything other than Scottish, despite having patently English surnames.

By the way, perhaps the greatest victory the Scots had over the English was the American War of Independence. Scots Presbyterians who had moved to Ulster felt discriminated against. Starting in 1714, they emigrated to North America. They became heavily involved in the creation of the United States. Eleven US presidents have Scottish ancestry by way of Ulster. Many Americans are proud of their 'Scotch-Irish' heritage.

Britannia was Scottish

Frances Theresa Stewart, granddaughter of Walter Stewart, First Lord Blantyre, was regarded as the most beautiful woman in England. Frances grew up in France where her father, also Walter Stewart, was court physician to Queen Henrietta Maria. In January 1662, at the age of 14, she came to the English court of Charles II as Maid of Honour to the king's wife, Katherine of Braganza.

Her beauty was quickly noticed. The diarist Samuel Pepys christened her 'La Belle Stewart'. Not least among her admirers was the king himself. Charles II was fond of his pleasures. One of his biographers, Ronald Hutton, described him: 'He was the playboy monarch, naughty but nice, the hero of all who prized urbanity, tolerance, good humour, and the pursuit of pleasure above the more earnest, sober, or martial virtues.'

Charles's contemporary, the Earl of Rochester, was less subtle. In a verse he wrote, 'Restless he rolls from Whore to Whore, A Merry Monarch, scandalous and poor' (and that's leaving out the rude bits). He entertained a constant stream of mistresses, from prostitutes to aristocrats. Perhaps most famous is Nell Gwynn, a working-class orange seller, turned actress, turned king's paramour. She bore him two children. Barbara Villiers bore him three. Then there was Hortense Mancini, known as the Italian Whore, and Louise de Kerouaille known as the French whore (when Nell Gwynn was mistaken by a crowd for Louise, she loudly informed them that she actually was 'the Protestant Whore'), just to mention a few.

La Belle Stewart from Blantyre was the king's lost love

But the one that got away was Frances Theresa Stewart. From her arrival at the Royal Court Charles pursued her and she resisted. He was not an easy man to resist. Ronald Hutton noted, 'the man was a seducer, in a much broader sense than that normally attributed to him … Charles possessed one of the most potent of all social assets, the ability to make every individual whom he encountered feel to be of special interest to him'.

It may be that her unobtainability was the aphrodisiac, but the king's passion for La Belle Stewart was fierce. It was observed that 'the King is now become besotted upon Mrs Stewart, that he gets into corners, and will be with her half an houre together kissing her to the observation of all the world', but still she let him no closer.

He wrote her a (not particularly good) poem:

But when I consider the truth of her heart,
Such an innocent passion, so kind without art,
I fear I have wronged her, and hope she may be

> So full of true love to be jealous of me.
> Oh then 'tis I think that no joys are above
> The pleasures of love.

He took part in a bizarre game in which Lady Castlemaine (another of Charles's lovers) persuaded Frances to take part in a pretend wedding ceremony where the two ladies were to wed each other. At the last minute Charles stepped into Lady Castlemaine's place.

When the queen fell ill, Frances was on his mind. A courtier noted that 'his doting is so great that it is verily thought if the Queene had died, he would have married her.'

How to flatter her so highly as to meet his ends? Charles made her the image of the nation. That image is familiar to us all. For those of us old enough to remember pre-decimalisation coinage it is an image we carried daily in our pockets. Frances Stewart became the model for Britannia.

Roman Emperors Hadrian (AD 117–138) and Antoninus Pius (AD 138–161) had both commemorated their achievements in Britain with striking coins featuring Britannia. She appeared holding a spear in her left hand with her left arm resting on a shield and her right foot on a pile of rocks. She had been quiet for 1,500 years. Now she emerged with the face of Frances Stewart. Samuel Pepys wrote, 'At my goldsmith's did observe the King's new meal, where, in little, there is Mrs Stuart's face as well-done as ever I saw anything in my whole life, I think: and a pretty thing it is, that he should choose her face to represent Britannia by'.

The Stewart Britannia first appeared on a medal and then on copper halfpennies and farthings. She remained on British coins until decimalisation in 1971 and even reappeared on the 50p piece in 2006.

Charles had immortalised her, but it did no good. In 1667 she did the unthinkable: she married someone else. She married the Duke of Redmond and Lennox, also called Charles Stewart.

The king was devastated, but allowed her to return to court. Ironically, it appears that only after she was married to another man, did she finally concede to the king.

By the way, Charles fathered at least fourteen illegitimate children, but not a single child in wedlock. Without a legal heir, his brother James took the throne, which led to a lot of bother.

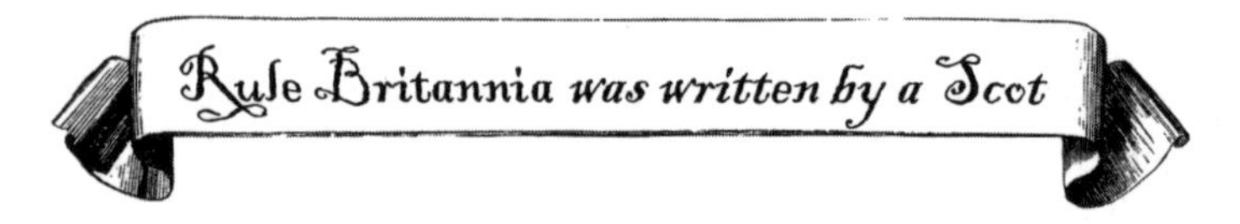

Rule Britannia was written by a Scot

The triumphant British anthem *Rule Britannia* was written by a Scot. James Thomson, from Ednam in the Borders, was pro-union. He wrote the rousing words to try to foster a sense of Britishness. They were first performed in 1740 in a play about Alfred the Great to a tune by Thomas Arne.

Though the song was written in support of George I's Hanoverian government, Bonnie Prince Charlie's supporters turned it into a pro-Jacobite song by the simple act of changing the words to 'Go brave hero, brave hero boldly go, and wrest thy sceptre from thy foe'.

The Jacobites also tried to appropriate *God Save the King* with:

God bless the prince, I pray,
God bless the prince I pray,
Charlie I mean.
That Scotland we may see
Freed from vile Presbyt'ry,
Both George and his Feckie,
Ever so, Amen.

('Feckie' was Frederick, Prince of Wales)

There was a Hanoverian backlash with the infamous words:

> Lord, grant that Marshal Wade,
> May by thy mighty aid,
> Victory bring.
> May he sedition hush,
> and like a torrent rush,
> Rebellious Scots to crush,
> God save the King.

This was a 'temporary' verse added to the national anthem at the time of the 'forty five'. It is remembered only by appalled Scottish Nationalists.

One of the outstanding legacies of the Jacobite rebellions, particularly Bonnie Prince Charlie's attempt, was a whole cannon of songs, many of which are still played in folk clubs and pub sessions.

By the way, the most widely accepted unofficial Scottish anthem was written in 1967. Celebrating the Battle of Bannockburn in 1314, it is commonly thought to be a traditional song, but was, in fact, written by Roy Williams of the Corries. Originally a contemplative song commemorating those that fell, it is now roared by thousands at rugby matches and other events.

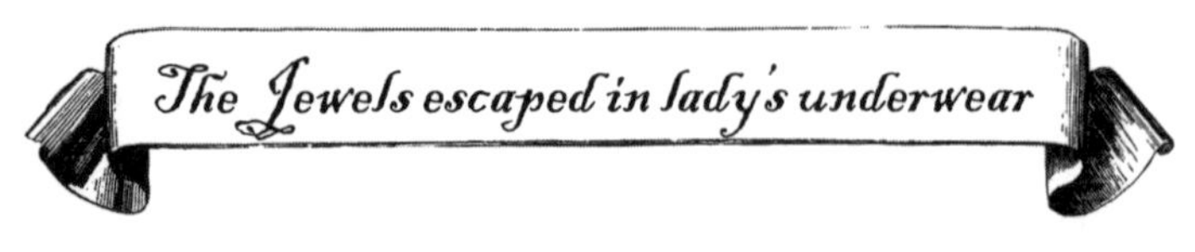

Dunnottar Castle has a long history dating back to Pictish times and a history of withstanding sieges. They withstood the attack of Æthelstan in the tenth century and held out bravely against Oliver Cromwell 700 years later.

Charles II, an exile and fugitive from England, was at least king of Scotland. He was crowned at Scone, in January 1651, in a ceremony that included the Honours of Scotland (the Scottish equivalent to the Crown Jewels of England). The Honours, a vital symbol of Scotland's monarchy, consisted of a crown, a ceremonial sword and a sceptre.

The Honours should have been returned to Edinburgh Castle, but Oliver Cromwell had seized Edinburgh, so the Honours were sent to Dunnottar Castle for safety. Dunnottar was the home of the Earls Marischal who were traditionally responsible for all ceremonial activities in the Scottish Court, including coronations, and with that the charge of protecting the Royal Honours, even though the Earl Marischal was in prison at the time the Honours came to Dunnottar. In any case, it was one of the few remaining Royalist strongholds.

Cromwell was keen to get his hands on the Honours; he hated them as a symbol of monarchy, but was also aware that he could sell them off to the highest bidder, as he had the English Crown Jewels.

Cromwell was determined to destroy the Honours as he had destroyed the English Crown Jewels. The Earl Marischal was taken prisoner by Cromwell, so the defence of Dunnottar was in the hands of Sir George Ogilvy of Barras when, in September 1651, the English troops appeared at Dunnottar and settled down to a long siege. The garrison of sixty-nine men held out through the long winter. By May 1652 Dunnottar Castle was the only place in Scotland where the royal flag still flew. But the English eventually brought in heavy guns and began to bombard the castle. For ten days the guns pounded the castle, and the number of defenders dwindled. Finally, after a siege lasting eight months in total, Ogilvy surrendered Dunnottar to Cromwell's men.

Missing Jewels

The English forces stripped the place seeking the royal regalia, but it was gone. There are two versions of events. The most colourful is that Mrs Grainger, wife of the minister at Kineff a few miles away, pleaded with the English officers. She was admitted to the castle to bring comfort to the women inside. She made her visit and was safely conducted away from the castle – with the Crown Jewels hidden in her underwear. Given the fashion for huge dresses, a crown and a sceptre seemed feasible, but how, we wondered, could she manage a 4.5ft-long sword? Then we discovered that the sword was broken in half for the escape, making the story at least feasible. We just wonder why she didn't clink.

The other version is that the Honours were lowered from the cliff in a basket where they were picked up by Mrs

Grainger, who was posing as a seaweed gatherer. The regalia were whisked back to Kineff church where they were hidden below the floorboards. It is said that Mrs Grainger took the items out of hiding every now and then to dry them out by the fire. After the Restoration they finally came out of hiding.

They came out of hiding only to be hidden away in a trunk in Edinburgh Castle, since after the Act of Union they had no practical role in the United Kingdom. (A new set of royal jewels were created for Charles II, to replace the ones flogged off by Cromwell.) They were not put on display until 1818, following a campaign by Sir Walter Scott, among others. They have been on display since then, apart from a period during the Second World War when they were taken away for safety.

They can be seen today in the Crown Room in Edinburgh Castle, alongside the Stone of Destiny. The crown is paraded in ceremonies in the Scottish Parliament. The sword and sceptre are regarded as too fragile to travel.

Scotland was famous for its pearls

The Crown of Scotland, in its present form, was created for James V around 1540. It contains many Scottish pearls, the largest of them known as the Kelly Pearl which came from the River Ythan. This was added to the crown by James VI when it was presented to him in 1621. Scottish pearls come from freshwater mussels and not from oysters. The most spectacular pearl of modern times is known as 'Little Willie', after its finder, William Abernathy. It was fished from the Tay in 1967 and sold to Cairncross jewellers in Perth. Scottish pearls have a long history (their quality was one of the reasons Julius Caesar cited as a reason for invading Britain), but in 1998 pearl fishing was banned. Apart from changing river conditions, a major factor in sending the Scottish pearl mussel plummeting towards extinction was wetsuit-clad amateurs who lacked the skills (and concerns for the stock) of the traditional pearl fishers, many of whom were travellers. The new breed stripped out whole beds of mussels, rather than having the knowledge to recognise the signs which would indicate that a particular shell would contain treasure.

Of the other Honours, the Italian-made sword was presented to James IV by Pope Julius IV in 1507 and the sceptre, made in 1494, was presented to James V by Pope Alexander VI. The three were first used together for the coronation of Mary, Queen of Scots.

Taken away by the fairies

In 1893 renowned folklorist Andrew Lang, from Selkirk, edited and published a book written over 200 years before. In his introduction he says of the book's author, the Revd Robert Kirk, 'He died (if he did die, which is disputed) in 1692 …'. There is a strong tradition of clergymen researching and recording history and traditions, even where these traditions stretch back to pagan beliefs and rituals and might seem to be a contradiction of the Church's teaching. Robert Kirk from Aberfoyle was one such clergyman. He was the seventh son of the minister. Following in the family tradition, he took up the cloth, studying theology at St Andrews and taking a masters degree at Edinburgh University. He became a minister at Balquidder before returning to his native kirk in Aberfoyle.

Robert Kirk was a minister and a ferocious scholar. He had a passion for spreading the Word of the Lord. He published the first translation of the metrical psalms into Gaelic. Apparently, when he discovered that the Synod of Argyll was engaged in the same enterprise at the same time as him, he drove himself relentlessly, working through the night so his would be completed first. He saw to the completion of the Gaelic translation of the Bible, begun earlier by Bishop William Bedell (and to its publication in 1690). It was funded by scientist Robert Boyle.

Robert Kirk was a scholar and a seventh son

Yet this same fervent Protestant was also passionate about investigating the precarious creatures – elves, fauns and fairies – that were part of a pagan past, but that had never quite gone away. He put great importance on the fact that he was born a seventh son, claiming that this gave him access to 'second sight', the ability to see what others could not. His life's work was *The Secret Commonwealth*, which was not to be published in his lifetime.

The work, written around 1691-92, was resurrected by two of Scotland's great champions of folklore. It was published in 1815 by Sir Walter Scott with the subtitle 'An essay of the nature and actions of the subterranean (and, for the most part) invisible people, heretofore going under the name of elves, faunes, and fairies, or the lyke among the low-country Scots, as they are described by those who have the second sight, and now to occasion further inquiry, collected and compared, by a circumspect inquirer residing among the Scottish-Irish in Scotland' and published again in 1893 by *Fairy Book* author Andrew Lang, with a more succinct title.

While in Lang's time the Physical Society in Edinburgh was actively investigating supernatural phenomenon (Lang mentions a survey in which 17,000 answers were considered) in Kirk's time such enquiries were a more dangerous affair. Belief in mystical creatures was widespread (Stone Age arrowheads were generally accepted to be from fairy weapons) and, while Scots enthusiasm for witch burning had waned, a trial for witchcraft was still a distinct possibility. Kirk's detailed knowledge of the fairies and elves would have been highly suspicious. Andrew Lang explains, 'Mr. Kirk… speaks of the *Sleagh Maith* as confidently as if he were discussing the habits of some remote race which he has visited'.

The Sleagh Maith (Gaelic for the good people) are the fairies. Kirk explains they are 'said to be of a middle nature betwixt man and angel ... of intelligent studious spirits, and light, changeable bodies (like those called astral) somewhat of the nature of a condensed cloud and best seen in twilight.' He described them with such detail as, 'Their apparel and speech is like that of the people and country under which they live ... they speak but little and that by way of whistling – clear, not rough'.

It was challenging for a minister to reveal that they have 'no discernible religion, love or devotion towards God ... they disappear whenever they hear his name invoked ...'. He does admit that the growing strength of Christian belief had led to the underground folk tending to keep more and more to themselves and that this was the reason for the decline in encounters with humans in recent times.

He notes that 'second sight', which he himself possessed, granted the ability to see fairies, but points out that this power is not connected with witchcraft. He explains that 'the derivation of it cannot always be wicked.'

In the essay he goes on to provide lots of information on the types of beings, their habits and lifestyles. This scholarly knowledge and sympathetic stance did not, it appears, go unnoticed by the fairies themselves.

Kirk was given to taking daily walks around Aberfoyle. His route took in a local Fairy Hill (of which there are many in Scotland). It was there he was found lying one morning, dead – or was he?

The funeral service was conducted. He was laid in the ground at Aberfoyle Kirk, but shortly afterward he appeared in a dream to a cousin and told him to contact Grahame of Duchray, another cousin. The instructions were, 'Say to Duchray, who is my cousin as well as your own, that I am not dead, but a captive in Fairyland; and only one chance remains for my liberation. When the posthumous child, of which my wife has been delivered since my disappearance, shall be brought to baptism, I will appear in the room, when, if Duchray shall throw over my head the knife or dirk which he holds in his hand, I may be restored to society; but if this is neglected, I am lost forever'.

True to his word Kirk appeared, but Duchray was so astonished by the apparition of the dead man walking that he failed to throw the knife. Kirk left, by the door, and has not been seen since. It is said that he had been taken to serve as chaplain to the Queen of the Fairies. His gravestone can be found in the kirkyard, but whether there is anything underneath it is another question.

'Yer Fauts I Maun Proclaim'

The eighteenth century was the age of enlightenment with great advances in science and philosophy. It was also a year of rebellion, with French and American revolutions. For many in Scotland the most colourful and iconic events were the failed Jacobite rebellions.

The Act of Union in 1707 merged Scotland with England in a new Great Britain. A few years later came the end of the Stuart occupancy of the Scottish and English thrones, officially. The Act of Settlement of 1701 stated that no Roman Catholic could become monarch. On Queen Anne Stuart's death a committee decided that George, Electorate of Brunswick-Luneburg, Hanover, great-grandson of James I was the next Protestant in line. Anne's brother, James Edward, felt he had a better claim.

James and his son pressed that claim in the Jacobite risings which are fondly remembered in many songs. They were hardly faultless. Robert Burns was something of a Jacobite sympathiser despite his republican tendency, but he was not uncritical:

> Ye Jacobites by name, yer fauts I maun proclaim,
>
> Yer doctrines I maun blame, you shall hear.

Bonnie Prince Charlie

The best remembered Scot of the eighteenth century is probably Bonnie Prince Charlie. He spent less than a year of his life in Scotland, yet his memory is celebrated in hundreds of songs in Gaelic, Scots and French. His image has appeared on millions of shortbread tins, tea towels and teacups. He was the leader of the campaign known as 'the Forty-five', a rebellion that intended to overthrow the German Hanoverian house which occupied the British throne in the person of George II. Charles's forces were the Jacobites (named after the Latin equivalent of James). They were against the Hanoverians; there were as many Scots against Charles as for him.

Charles's Jacobite Rebellion of 1845 is so deeply ingrained in Scottish memory that it is often remembered simply as 'the Forty-five'. But we should also remember 'the Zero-eight', 'the Fifteen', 'the Nineteen' and even 'the Fifty-nine' (which didn't actually happen). The Jacobites, for half a century, were nothing if not persistent.

The Old Pretender's war was over before
he was even in the country

Bonnie Charlie's father, James Frances, had only managed three months in the country. In 1715 he arrived in Scotland after the battles; his army was in disarray and the war was over before he got there. The biggest showdown was the Battle of Sherrifmuir, just north of Stirling. Both armies claimed to have won. Perhaps the best legacy of the battle was the song by Robert Burns, 'the Battle of Sherramuir', which elegantly tells the story from both sides. James Frances Edward Stewart retreated to Italy empty-handed, but was recognised by some on the continent, including the Pope, as King James VIII of Scotland and James III of England – just not in Scotland or England.

By the way, it is suspected that James thought about bringing up Charlie as a Protestant to increase his chances of getting back on the throne. The fact that they were living in Rome didn't make this easy.

We almost told him not to come!

James Frances named his son Charles Edward Louis Casimer Sylvester Severino Maria Stuart. We know him as Bonnie Prince Charlie, (maybe he should have gone with Maria instead of Betty in the cross-dressing episode).

Charlie was appointed Prince Regent and charged with regaining the throne for his father. In 1744 Scotland wasn't on the agenda – King of England was the big prize; King of Scotland and Ireland would be thrown in. Charlie was supposed to arrive on the English coast with a substantial French army. After a storm threw the fleet into disarray the French delayed and delayed and eventually abandoned the scheme. Charlie, now without an army, swore that he would come 'even though with a single footman'.

The possibility of an attack through Scotland was up for discussion. Jacobite sympathisers met at the 'Buck Club' in Edinburgh and discussed the matter. Opinion was divided. Murray of Broughton was among those who urged caution. A vote was taken and a letter drawn up. It told the prince that unless he came with 6,000 troops, arms for 10,000 more and 30,000 Louis D'Or in cash, he was bound to fail. Another Charles Stuart, 5th Earl of Traquair, was charged with taking the letter to London and there finding a courier to take it to Charlie in France.

The earl was distracted by a visit to Teresa Conyers, a lady he had taken a fancy to, and four months later turned up in Edinburgh with the letter still in his possession. Another messenger was sent, but by that time Charlie had left Paris.

Charles Edward Steward invaded
Scotland with a force of seven men

Charles arrived on a remote island in the Hebrides, Eriskay, with just seven men (two Scots, one English and four Irish). They became known as the 'Seven Men of Moidart'.

By the way, in the nineteenth century seven beech trees were planted to commemorate the seven men. Only two and a half are still standing.

The one contribution he did get from France was the Irish. Irish mercenaries serving France were to come to his aid (only one battalion and some cavalry did turn up, but they made a significant contribution to the campaign).

Glenfinnan, the rallying point for the clans to come to support Charlie, has a resonance in the mythology of the rebellion. The Highlanders 'threw their bonnets in the air and huzza'd... crying aloud, "Long live King James VIII and Charles, Prince of Wales. Prosperity to Scotland and no union".'

It was a bit of a damp squib. Only a few of the clans turned up on time, but the fire was lit and Highlanders trickled in. By the time he got to Prestonpans he had 5,000 men. Once they got south of the Borders thousands of English Jacobites would surely rally to the cause.

Taking Edinburgh was easy

Edinburgh was easy. The propaganda says that cheering crowds greeted him (though why the seat of the Scottish reformation should turn out for a Catholic invader is not entirely explained). Edinburgh Castle kept its gates locked. Charlie didn't try to take it with any great effort. Instead he met the English army, sent north to rout him, at nearby Prestonpans. In any game an early goal is a great confidence booster. Charlie got his here. The battle took fifteen minutes before John Cope, the English commander, turned tail. The song says, 'Hey Johnny Cope, are ye waulkin' yet?'

By the way, the Battle of Prestonpans is celebrated in a tapestry longer than the Bayeux Tapestry. The work, which is strictly speaking an embroidered fabric rather than a woven tapestry, was completed in 2010. The impressive artwork has toured Scotland and France and was the inspiration for the 'Great Tapestry of Scotland'.

Marching south, Charlie's army got as far as Derby before things went wrong. We've seen the decision to turn north described as 'inexplicable'. He was on his front foot with a few early goals; surely the game was in the bag – but this was to be a game of two halves.

'Ruined and betrayed' by his own men

At Derby a difference of ambition reared its head. The Scottish support was happy to place a Catholic Stuart on the throne of Scotland, but England? The thought of marching into London with a few thousand men was beyond them. The theory that legions of latent Catholic Englishmen would flock to their cause simply didn't happen. For the Highlanders, Scotland was plenty. They would go no further.

Charlie's eyes were always on the prize of the English crown. He was not for turning back. The argument raged. 'You ruin and betray me if you do not go on,' he cried; only the Irish supported him. Then stepped in another Irishman, Dudley Bradstreet, something of a chancer. He arrived at the camp, eager to join the Stuart cause. He brought intelligence. There was an army of 9,000 in place, north of London, waiting for Charlie's approach. It was enough to swing the argument. No such army existed, but the news of it was enough. Charlie conceded to his generals' opinion. They turned back to Scotland.

Needing a strong base in Scotland (having failed to take Edinburgh Castle on the way south) they besieged Stirling Castle. A Hanoverian force was sent to relieve the castle. Charlie's forces intercepted them in an open battle on Falkirk Muir. And won! It was the last score they were going to make.

Three months later came the Battle of Culloden. It was the last full-pitched battle ever fought in Britain. For Charlie it was an ignominious defeat. For the Highlanders that had supported him this last year it was a disaster. For Highland culture and the clan system it was a death sentence.

Charlie ignored the advice of the same generals who he felt had abandoned him at Derby when it came to choosing a battlefield. His troops were knackered from an abortive attempt to surprise the enemy camp the night before.

The government troops had devised a bayonet drill to defeat the feared 'Highland Charge' which had overwhelmed them at Prestonpans. The drill took courage and trust. The Highlanders would run headlong at them with a targe (small shield) on their left arms to deflect bayonets, then they would either get them with the sword or axe in their right hands or the dagger behind the shield in their left hands. The strategy developed required nerves of steel. It was an individual, personal, outflanking manoeuvre. You, as a soldier in the line, were to pay no attention to the fearsome warrior rushing at you. Your job was to stick your bayonet into the side of the Highlander who was attacking your pal on the left, next to you in the line. When the Highlander raised his shield against your mate he was wide open from the side. That was your target. You could only pray that the guy on your right had read the memo.

Charlie's army were mostly Highlanders with the Irish battalion, a few Irish cavalry and a few Lowlanders and English. The Hanoverian commander, the Duke of Cumberland (known as 'Butcher' Cumberland), had English men with some Germans and Austrians and a battalion from Ulster. Plus he had four battalions of Lowland Scots and even some Highlanders. This wasn't simply English against Scots.

Charlie lost.

Charlie escaped wearing a maid's dress

Next came a humiliating retreat for the prince. The man was used to the fine courts of Italy and France, yet here he was, dragged through the Highlands' caves and bothies, lucky to have porridge. A common fugitive. He spent part of the journey in skirts, dressed as Betty Burke, serving maid to Flora MacDonald. When he was challenged on Skye that Betty did not walk, talk or behave like a woman, Flora explained that this was because she was Irish. The explanation sufficed and Charlie made it to a boat and back to France. He was exiled from France as part of an Anglo–French peace treaty a few years later.

By the way, Charlie wasn't the first Jacobite to escape in a frock. In 1716 William Maxwell, 5th Earl of Nithsdale, was smuggled out of the Tower of London on the eve of his execution dressed as a woman. In an elaborate plan his wife, Winnifred, organised a succession of lady visitors to his cell. The guards failed to notice that three women had come out when only two had gone in and that one, particularly distraught, lady had kept a hankie over her face. William made it free to France.

The government set about dismantling the clan system with brutality and with legislation designed to end the Highland way of life.

Charles drowned his sorrows in alcohol and never achieved his father's acknowledgement as king. His time in Scotland was brief. His campaign was a failure: the result a disaster for the Highlands. Yet he is remembered as a Scottish hero. Strange but true.

By the way, Flora MacDonald, after a brief stay in the Tower of London, married. She and her husband, Hugh MacDonald of Skye, travelled to America where he fought in the War of Independence, on the British side.

Close the gate on your way out!

An impressive set of gates were closed after Prince Charlie passed through them. A promise was made that they wouldn't be opened again until a Stuart monarch sat on the throne. The gates are the Bear Gates at Traquair House in the Borders. Traquair is the oldest continuously inhabited house in Scotland. It has an impressive history dating back to the twelfth century and possibly earlier. It was established as a hunting lodge in the Ettrick Forest for the Scottish Royals.

In the eighteenth century it was owned by a branch of the Stuarts that maintained the Catholic faith. The house has an elaborately disguised 'priest room' to allow clergy to escape detection. They were natural supporters of the Jacobite cause. The fourth earl, Charles Stuart, was imprisoned for his part in the 1715 rising. The fifth earl, also Charles Stuart, welcomed Prince Charles Stuart on his way south, flushed with his success at Prestonpans. The promise was made and the gates have remained closed ever since.

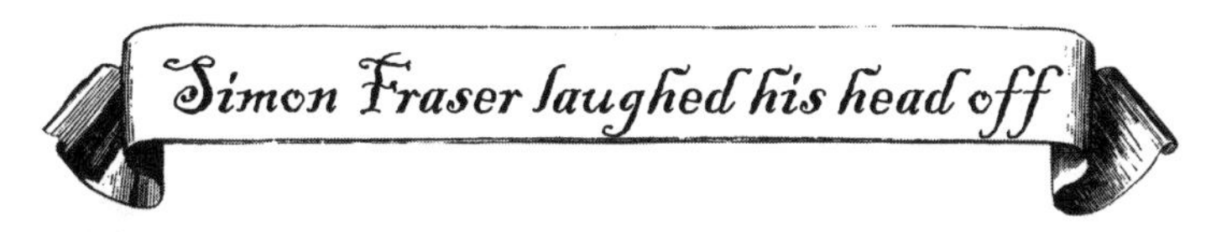

Simon Fraser laughed his head off

Simon Fraser, 11th Lord Lovat, was a prominent Jacobite executed for his beliefs, despite the fact that he had a reputation for changing sides. In 1715 he had stood with King George and the Hanoverians against the Jacobites, while in 1745 he followed Prince Charlie and fought beside him on the losing side at Culloden. He had switched back and forth in various intrigues in the intervening years – Jacobite, Hanoverian, Protestant, Catholic – whatever suited the moment. The best that could be said was that he was treacherous to both parties.

After Culloden he was a wanted man. Castle Downie was raided and his wine collection was stolen as the buildings burned. He was captured on an island on Loch Morar where he was hidden in a tree. In his five-day trial it was a fellow Jacobite, John Murray of Broughton, who gave evidence against him. Known as a rapist, bigamist and cheat, Fraser could hardly expect much sympathy, even from his own clan. He was described as 'the most detested man in his Country' and it was also said that, 'By his public life, he has left an indelible stain upon the honour of the Highland character, upon his party, upon his country'.

His death was inevitable but also strange. Just before his execution on Tower Hill in April 1747, a scaffold which had been built to house spectators collapsed, leaving twenty people dead. Fraser thought this was hilarious and is said to have still been laughing when the axe fell. This may be the origin of the phrase 'laughing your head off'. He was the last man to be publicly beheaded in England.

The Bute tsunami

It was 1755, ten years after the great Jacobite rising, when the 'king o'er the water' came o'er the water to enter a competition for the crown, with much blood and mayhem along the way.

The campaign pretty much passed the Isle of Bute by, except for the pulpit of Kingarth church. The minister, one James Stewart, was also laird of Kinwhinlick. The church position had been kept vacant for fourteen years until James had completed sufficient education to take the pulpit.

In the years following 1740 he prayed for the Bonnie Prince's return. In 1745 he prayed fervently for the prince's success and in the years following he would not let it go. His pro-Jacobite views were a familiar theme, well known to the Christian folk of Kingarth parish.

Of course these treacherous remarks did not go un-noticed, but James's enemies in the authorities bided their time, until a fit case could be brought against him. The charge they found was arson! This for merely evicting tenants using the time-honoured method of burning their houses down. Yet his congregation loyally turned out on the shore in November 1755 to wish him farewell.

A few in the crowd noticed the tide ebbing far faster and further than normal. Then the water came back in a rushing wave, hitting the shoreline and pushing on over the dry land. It brought boats with it, throwing them up onto the land. All agreed that this was the wrath of heaven. Wrath expressed over the ill treatment of their minister.

A wider view might see that, whatever His anger over events in Bute, elsewhere bore the brunt: an earthquake 150 miles off Lisbon on 1 November 1755 created a tsunami which killed over 50,000 people in Portugal, Spain and Morocco.

Named after a Spanish province

We had wondered for some time how a small village in the Scottish Borders came to be named after a province in southern Spain. In 2005 we got to find out. We were engaged to run a community project. As well as experiencing a great children's festival we investigated some of the local legends. One that stood out was the connection between the village and Admiral Thomas Cochrane, 'Le Loup de Mer', inspiration for the Captain Aubrey novels and the film *Master and Commander*.

The investigation of the Cochrane family is an example of just how rich Scotland's history is and how one family can contain an array of eccentric characters and strange but true events. Such great stories are out there in every city, town and village.

We established that the property, previously Romanno Grange, was indeed bought in 1726, and named 'Lamancha' by Major Thomas Cochrane, but not the admiral – his grandfather, the 8th Earl of Dundonald. He regarded Lamancha as a second home and the family kept a property there for some years.

Certainly we discovered that La Loup de Mare visited the house as a child, being a cousin of the Lamancha Cochranes. This was a bit disappointing, however we equally discovered how many strange but true stories could be found in one small village, indeed in one family.

After the major's death the title passed to his eldest son Archibald, but the house was put on the market and bought by the ninth son, Alexander. Sir Alexander Forrester Inglis Cochrane followed the family tradition by joining the navy.

There followed a distinguished career in places such as Martinique and America. After the American War of Independence he spent several quiet years in retirement. It was not to last. Renewal of hostilities with France saw him back in action in 1790, in command of HMS *Thetis*, with 42 guns and 261 men. Of these men five others were Cochranes –all related to Alexander.

He was to die suddenly, in Paris, on 26 January 1832, surrounded by his grandchildren and with his daughter and one of his brothers at his side.

A Spanish troubador

Alexander's son, born aboard ship, was to prove something of an eccentric. Captain Charles Stuart Cochrane, at first a dutiful son, entered naval service and like many of his family served during the Napoleonic Wars. On leaving naval service he turned to travel, seeking adventure. He travelled up the Magdalena River in Columbia hoping to make his fortune through copper-mining under the patronage of Simon Bolivar. He was unsuccessful but his adventures during that period formed the basis of the book he was later to write.

It was his behaviour during his return to Scotland that marked him as eccentric: he adopted the alias 'Senor Juan de Vega' and, describing himself as a Spanish minstrel, took to the roads of Britain and Ireland strumming his guitar and singing for his supper. Not usual, or acceptable, behaviour for a member of the famous Cochrane family and we can only wonder if his family's long-term interest in Spain had had an effect on him.

After a prolonged sojourn around the Scottish Borders – during which we might assume that he visited Lamancha – he revealed his true identity to Edinburgh society, upon which he was judged to be 'a bit cracked'! In fact this was not true, as proven by his invention of a machine for spinning fine cashmere which was later to win an award. He set up a mill in Glasgow and was to remain there while he penned his two Colombian travel books and the 'Journal of a tour made by Senor Juan de Vega, a Spanish Minstrel, of 1828-29, through Great Britain and Ireland'.

But it was Alexander's brother, Charles's uncle, who was to be the real family embarrassment.

Andrew James Cochrane Johnstone made it clear that he intended to break with family tradition and would not follow the naval career that had marked the Cochrane family males for generations. His father was displeased when he chose a career in the army – and a very rich wife! On his marriage to Lady Georgiana Johnstone he added her surname to his own, perhaps as a reminder of the circles in which he now moved.

Having achieved the rank of colonel at age 30, his career was not to be marked with the glory of his naval father, cousins and nephews. He was appointed Governor of St Dominica in the West Indies where a cousin (named only as A. Cochrane) described his rule as 'one marked with tyranny, extortion and vice … and he drove a brisk trade in Negroes and kept a harem'. He was eventually court-martialled, but on his return to England he used his influence (and that of his wife) to secure a seat in Parliament.

His brother Alexander, by now an admiral, helped him attain a further appointment in the West Indies where he 'again ran riot, gun-running and swindling on a massive scale'. If these shaming acts were appalling to society and to the majority of his family, the worst was yet to come. In his final criminal act before fleeing to the Continent for the remainder of his life, he was to implicate his nephew and besmirch one of the most admirable careers of the entire Cochrane family.

In 1814 Andrew James hatched a stock-market scam that involved a bogus Royalist announcing the death of Napoleon, causing a fluctuation on the market which he turned to his advantage. Andrew implicated his nephew, the famous Admiral Thomas Cochrane, in this fraud and almost ruined his career. Although almost certainly innocent of all charges, the admiral was tried (a travesty of a trial), found guilty and stripped of his knighthood. He was fined £1,000 which he refused to pay; was sentenced to a time in the pillory, which he managed to avoid; and was imprisoned. In spite of strong public support, it took Lord Cochrane seventeen years to get a full pardon. He was eventually reinstated in the navy as a Rear Admiral. His uncle had escaped to the Continent and never returned.

Naval hero

Thomas Cochrane (the famous one) was born in 1775 at Annesfield in Lanarkshire to Archibald Cochrane, ninth Earl of Dundonald, and spent much of his early years in Culross in Fife. His connection with the house at Lamancha is largely though his childhood visits to his grandmother, the widow of Major Thomas Cochrane, where he was noted as adventurous and full of pranks.

After a formal education he entered his naval career aged 18 as a mid-shipman aboard his Uncle Alexander's frigate *The Hind*. Within three years he was a lieutenant, worshipped by his men, and said to be one of the most daring and fearless commanders of the entire British fleet. He was to continue his naval career-winning plaudit after plaudit for his actions all over the world, but it was as master and commander of his ship *The Speedy* that he was to be immortalised. In this sloop he fought and captured *El Gamo*, a Spanish frigate, three times her firepower. In this same ship he went on to capture many enemy ships in the Mediterranean.

He quickly rose through the ranks and also became an MP, until the 1814 scandal. His period of disfavour at home did not hamper his naval activities. In 1818 he took command of the Chilean Navy and aided the independence of both Chile and Peru. In 1823 he commanded the Brazilian Navy in their struggle to free themselves from Portuguese control. By 1827 he was fighting with the Greeks against the Ottoman Empire.

After his return to grace he went on to have a long – and largely distinguished career – commanding the West Indies and America station until 1851. In 1854, at the age of 80, he was deeply disappointed not to have been given a command in the Crimean War.

Admiral Cochrane married the same woman three times

But perhaps his personal eccentricities are less well known. It is frequently recorded that Thomas was a man of passions: passionate about the navy, his men and their welfare and safety, politics, social injustice and many other things. A striking, handsome, red-haired man standing 6ft 2in tall, he found his greatest passion in Katherine (Kitty) Barnes, whom he had first seen standing in a school playground when she was 16 years old and he was 37. Always a man of action, he promptly eloped with her to Dumfriesshire where they were married at the Queensberry Arms Hotel. They were to marry two more times! He married her again in an Anglican church in Tunbridge Wells (1818) and finally in the Church of Scotland in Edinburgh (1825).

'Marry her!' roared Cochrane, 'I would marry her in a hundred churches. I would marry her all over the world ... I am ready to marry her in every church in London. I would do it a thousand times.'

But Kitty thought he was overdoing it, 'There was no end of marrying me... I was so tired of being married.'

Perhaps Kitty had a droll sense of humour, or perhaps she was simply tired. She followed him all over the world, giving him a daughter and four sons. The eldest, Thomas Barnes Cochrane, was to succeed to the title of Earl of Dundonald.

In South America his name is still revered. In Spain he is now regarded as a national hero for his actions against the French. In 2005 the town of Roses, in Catalonia, dedicated a plaque to Thomas: 'Le Loup de Mer', Wolf of the Sea, for his defence of their town in 1808.

Mungo Park, a farmer's son from Foulshiels near Selkirk, trained as a doctor at Edinburgh University. In 1795, at the age of 24, he set off on an expedition into the dark heart of Africa. The trip, funded by the African Association, aimed to track the course of the River Niger.

Setting off with a few local guides, he soon ran into trouble. He was caught in local strife between Moroccan warlords Ali and King Daisy (really). Mungo was taken prisoner by Ali and 'barbarously treated'. He was starved and kept short of water. He escaped, was recaptured, escaped again, was robbed by Moors, who took even his cloak, and went on the run.

He needed to keep under cover but also needed to find water and food. He drank from a pool full of huge frogs which frightened his horse. He risked begging for food at native settlements and was turned away until an old woman took him in. He was ordered to leave by the local King Mansong. He abandoned his horse when it fell ill, only to find it again. He was pursued by a lion. He proceeded down the River Niger again and was sent away from many places. He was robbed of his clothes and horse. He finally found a friendly reception from a Chief Mansa, but fell ill with fever and it was many months before he could continue. He eventually made it to the sea and sailed home. In spite of all odds he had survived.

His account of the journey, *Travels in the Interior of Africa*, was a success and is now rated as a classic. Safely back in the Borders he married his childhood sweetheart and set up a comfortable doctor's practice in Peebles.

We, the authors, can in no way support Mr Park's opinions, especially since we live in Peebles, in fact about 50 yards from the site of his surgery. But, Mungo Park was bored.

A friend reported his opinion to the *Scots Magazine*, 'a few inglorious winters of practice at Peebles was a risk as great, and would tend as effectually to shorten life as the journey which he was about to undertake'. After all he had suffered on the first trip, and all the comforts of Peebles, he was back off to Africa.

In 1805 he set off to explore the Niger, better financed and equipped. He had an officer and thirty-seven men. By the time they reached the river only eleven survived; by the time a boat was finally constructed to sail east they were down to three.

In his last letter to the British Colonial Office he wrote:

> I shall set sail for the east with the fixed resolution to discover the termination of the Niger or perish in the attempt. Though all the Europeans who are with me should die, and though I were myself half dead, I would still persevere, and if I could not succeed in the object of my journey, I would at least die on the Niger.

This was prophetic. The details of his last days were uncovered by a later expedition. It appears that he and his remaining party drowned when their boat overturned during an attack by a large band of spear-carrying natives. But at least he wasn't in Peebles!

Mungo Park's travelling trunk has returned to the Borders

In 2015 a travelling trunk used by Park came on the market in New Zealand. The case had been left in Selkirk and was used by a later member of the Park family, quite sensibly, as a travelling trunk when he sailed to New Zealand. The trunk stayed there and found its way into the hands of a Maori chieftain. When it was auctioned, funds raised by private donations were available to bid for and win the lot. It is now on display in Halliwell House Museum in Selkirk along with related objects.

Mungo medals

The Royal Scottish Geographical Society has awarded the Mungo Park Medal annually since 1930. The medal is awarded for an outstanding contribution to geographical knowledge through exploration or adventure in potentially hazardous physical or social environments. Recipients have included Thor Heyerdhal, John Ridgeway, Kate Adie and Ray Mears.

By the way, the first winner was Captain Angus Buchanan, born in Orkney in 1886. He explored a region in Africa close to where Mungo Park had come to grief over 100 years before. Buchanan wrote in his 1921 book *Exploration of Air: Out of the World North of Nigeria*, 'I did not meet a single Englishman or Scot ... It can easily be understood why British Europeans do not make the journey ... if one can realise the desolation of that country and the exhausting heat of the African sun.' This certainly confirms that Mungo did indeed pursue his adventure in 'potentially hazardous physical or social environments'.

An Age of Change

Culloden was the last pitched battle fought on British soil. The conflict between Scotland and England had ended. The Highlanders who had followed the Catholic Prince Charlie gradually converted to Protestantism (except for Barra, Benbecula and South Uist, which retain a Catholic majority to this day). In the nineteenth century, Victoria was to take the throne.

Peace had come, except that during Victoria's reign were the First and Second Afghan Wars, the China Wars, the First and Second Sikh Wars, the Maori Wars, the Cape Frontier Wars, the Crimean War, the Ashanti Wars, the Zulu War, the Transvaal Rebellion, the Egypt and the Sudan Wars and the Boer War. Many Scottish soldiers, officers and men fought solidly for the British Empire.

The nineteenth century was an age of industrial revolution, an age of prosperity and an age of workhouses and cholera.

The great alarm

The last 'total war', the Napoleonic War, ended in 1815. It would be ninety-nine years before European powers would again face each other on European soil.

Hume Castle is an unusual-looking medieval Scottish castle because most of the stones and mortar to be seen are a folly created towards the end of the eighteenth century. However, the castle does have a long history dating back to the thirteenth century at least, and has a long association with the Home Clan.

The family are variously known as Home, or Hume, or Home pronounced Hume, and the clan is often referred to as Home/Hume. There is a story that whilst leading his men into the Battle of Flodden, Sir Alexander Home shouted out his family battle cry 'A Home, A Home', at which some of the troops turned tail, thinking he had ordered a retreat. This led to the change in pronunciation. The story is not verified on the Clan Home website.

The confusion in name continues with two more recent family sons: Sir Alex Douglas-Home (pronounced Hume) was British Prime Minister in the 1960s; Allan Octavian Hume was one of the founding spirits of the Indian National Congress (which eventually led India out of British rule) and in 1885 served as its first secretary.

Standing within sight of the English border, Castle Hume has been no stranger to conflict as campaigns proceeded north and south. It has at various times been in English hands for prolonged periods. Perhaps the greatest damage occurred in 1651 when Cromwell's troops, having achieved the surrender of the castle, chose to destroy it with explosives rather than hold it.

The 3rd Lord Marchmont, a Home, bought it in 1770 and created the structure we see today. One of its great stories, not to say embarrassments, was still to come. In 1804 the country was poised ready for invasions by Napoleon's forces. The technology to signal the arrival of the attack was ancient and well tried – beacon fires. The fires were stationed along the coast, each in sight of the previous one and the next. A lit beacon would send the signal racing up the coast.

On the night of 31 January 1804 a sergeant in the Berwickshire Volunteers saw the vital flames light up and ordered his beacon at Hume Castle to be lit. The signal went and 3,000 volunteers poured into the night ready to fend off Boney's invasion.

What, it turned out, the sergeant had seen were the fires from charcoal burners on the Cheviot Hills. There was no fleet and no invasion. The incident was christened 'the Great Alarm'.

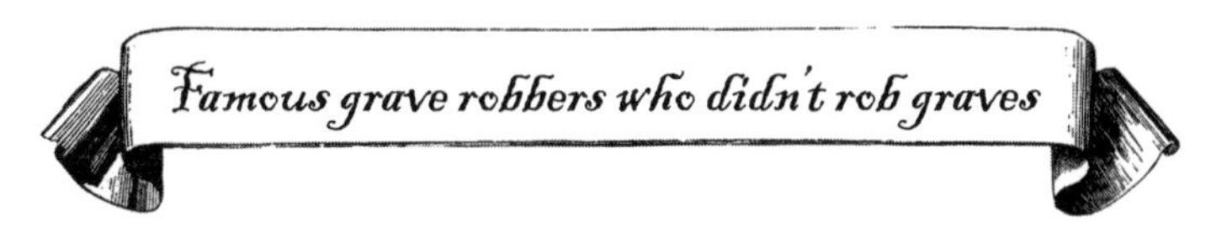

William Burke was from County Donegal in Ireland, and William Hare was probably from County Down. Both men came to Scotland seeking labouring work. Both worked as navvies digging the canal system, but they didn't meet until the start of 1828. In the course of that single year their activities made them famous as 'Burke and Hare, Body Snatchers!'

There was a great demand for dead bodies for research and teaching student surgeons. The legal supply was limited so it was supplemented by illegal means. Gangs would enter graveyards in the dead of night and remove freshly buried corpses from their graves. This led to a variety of preventative measures such as guards in graveyards or Mort Safes (these were metal cages locked over graves long enough for the body to have rotted until it was no longer an attractive proposition to recover, usually about six weeks).

Burke and Hare came to supply the hospitals' demand, but they did not dig up a single corpse. They found a novel way to find 'subjects' – murder. Their first corpse, Old Donald, died of natural causes. Hare and his wife Margaret, or Maggie, ran a boarding house in the West Bow of Edinburgh's Grassmarket. William Burke came to stay as a lodger. An elderly lodger

passed away owing considerable back rent (he had been due to pick up his annual army pension, but now this would not be forthcoming). Hare had already ordered the coffin to take him away, so it is likely that it was Burke who suggested selling his body to recover the rent.

The two men went to Edinburgh's Surgeon's Square where they met eminent surgeon Dr Robert Knox and several students, one of whom was William Ferguson, later to be Sir William Ferguson, Queen Victoria's doctor. The matter was discussed and the corpse duly delivered. A price of £7 10*s* was paid. It was a fortune for the two men.

The first murder was an 'act of mercy'

Their next opportunity came when a second lodger, Joseph, became ill. He had the fever and Hare's wife was naturally anxious to get him out of the house. Burke and Hare somehow agreed that a spot of euthanasia was called for. They smothered the old man with a pillow and got their second fee from the good doctor. This launched a spree which would see at least sixteen people murdered by the end of the year.

They quickly developed an effective *modus operandi*. They would lure people into the lodging house and entertain them with copious amounts of whisky. When they had passed out, or were sufficiently insensible, they would smother them. One of them would use one hand to close the mouth and nose, while the other held the victim's legs to stop them struggling. The bodies were then carted off in barrels to the surgeon. It was a profitable enterprise, but after a while they started getting rash. Towards the end some have said that they looked as if they wanted to be caught. Certainly Burke was so haunted by visions of their work that he couldn't sleep without a candle burning with a bottle of whisky inside him and another by his bed.

Burke, on one occasion, came across a police constable taking a drunken woman to the station. Burke, by all accounts a charmer, persuaded the policeman that he would save him trouble and would himself take care of the lady. He did indeed 'take care of her'.

The murder of Mary Patterson turned into a fiasco. Burke turned up with two young ladies. After one of them left, Burke's common-law wife Helen MacDougal attacked him for flirting with this very pretty girl. MacDougal left and Hare arrived. Mary was dispatched in the usual manner. The other girl, Janet Brown, turned up looking for her friend. Burke concocted a story that she had met a packman and decided to go to Glasgow with him. MacDougal reappeared, still in a jealous rage. An argument ensued while Mary Patterson was lying dead just a few feet away in the next room.

Things got no better when they got the body to the doctor's. Knox was so taken with the pretty corpse that he sent for an artist who drew the corpse in the pose of Venus. The problem for Burke and Hare was that they had previously drawn victims from the lower classes. Mary was low class but her profession allowed her to meet and deal with men of a higher class. She was a prostitute. In Surgeon's Square she was immediately recognised by at least two of the students. It is likely that they were former clients of the dead girl. One said that he had seen a girl standing in the Grassmarket and that she and this girl were 'as like as two peas in a pod'. Burke explained that she had died of drink and had been sold to them by an old woman. The young doctors did nothing to pursue the matter.

Big mistakes

James Wilson was a big mistake too. Known as Daft Jamie, he was a 'simpleton' who was a well-known character in the area. Killing him had been a struggle since he refused drink and was a strong lad. At the doctor's he was recognised straight away, but Knox denied this, quickly removing Jamie's head and distinctive club foot.

Their next murder, Mary Docherty, was their final error. Mr and Mrs Grey, lodgers in the guest house, became suspicious and went to the police. Burke, Hare, Margaret and Helen were arrested.

The authorities quickly recognised that they had a problem: lack of evidence. They only had one body, the last. The others had been skilfully and meticulously dismembered by the surgeons. The one that they did have showed no signs of assault (the smothering technique left the bodies without a mark, always a good selling point). The doctors would not admit that there was any evidence of foul play.

The public were baying for blood and yet Burke and Hare might walk free. Something had to be done. Sir William Rae, the Lord Advocate, approached Hare and asked him to turn King's Evidence – he could incriminate Burke and walk away. Hare grabbed at the chance.

Curiously, Hare's account, the account which saw Burke swing on the gallows, went missing and there is no record of his statement. Burke, on the other hand, sang like a canary. He gave a full confession and an extended interview to the Edinburgh newspaper the *Courant*. These can readily be accessed. What we know of the pair's exploits is from Burke's point of view. Hare's story is not known.

A strong reason for Burke's openness was his plea that his love, Helen MacDougal, had never been involved. MacDougal got off with the unique Scottish verdict of 'not proven' (which some have defined as 'Innocent, but don't do it again!'). Burke was convicted and sentenced. A crowd of 25,000 turned out in the Grassmarket to see him hang. This same mob was furious that Margaret and William Hare were to be freed. Daft Jamie's family tried to launch a private prosecution. Hare was smuggled out of Edinburgh.

When the coach stopped at a coaching inn in Lamancha in the Borders, Hare was recognised. Word went ahead and there was a mob 9,000-strong waiting for him in Dumfries. Again he was smuggled away. His consequent movements are a matter of speculation.

Burke entered the language as the word 'burker' for body snatchers or gravediggers with 'burking' as their activity. Of course we know that Burke and Hare had no part in such goings on – they were merely murderers.

A doctor's comeuppance

In the activities of Burke and Hare the medical staff were complicit. They never asked questions as to the origins of the corpses and even when there were clear indications that something was awry, for example with Mary Patterson or Daft Jamie, they took no action. While they suffered a certain amount of public displeasure, no charges were ever brought against them.

A doctor in Aberdeen was paid back for dealing in illegal corpses in a more direct fashion. The lovely story was published in the *Fife Journal* in 1829, when the deeds of Burke and Hare were fresh in the public mind.

It seems that an English ship returning from America berthed in Aberdeen. After the long sea crossing, the crew partook of some strong drink. When the conversation turned to the body trade and particularly the lack of justice for the doctors, a plan was hatched:

> A daring man of colour volunteered to be the subject, provided they could furnish him with a large knife. Being equipped with one of a proper size, he was put into a sack which had been procured; and three of the crew of the best address, called at the house of a Lecturer on Anatomy and disposed of the body, telling him it was one of their messmates who, previous to their arrival, had died of apoplexy. Having got £3 in hand, with the promise of more next day, they carried the corpse down into the cellar, the lecturer and his servant coming along with them and locking the door.

The African cut his way out of the sack and was waiting for the doctor. When the attack came the doctor fled, pursued by the corpse he had come down to examine. No matter how much a man of science and reason he may have been, we cannot help but wonder how much the legends of Black Nick, the Devil himself, rang through the man's mind.

The sailor returned to his companions and 'the whole crew, gloriously fu', returned to their vessel, which sailed next morning.

Body snatchers saved a woman's life

An activity as bizarre as grave digging inspires many stories. The grave diggers were also known as resurrection men or resurrectionists. In one case, at least, the term came close to the truth.

In the village of Chirnside in the Borders, a young minister moved to the parish with his young wife. Shortly afterwards he was devastated when his love took ill and died. Her funeral took place and she was buried in the local graveyard. A pretty young corpse was likely to fetch a good price. The temptation was too great and a party of resurrectionists turned up that night.

In the course of the exhumation one of the party noticed a ring on her finger. When he couldn't remove the ring he took his knife and sliced off the finger. The girl's eyes opened and stared at him. The shock had been enough to rouse her from her catatonic state. The rogues fled at some speed. The young woman made her way back to the manse. She appeared at the door in a shroud covered in blood: her husband fainted on the spot. The story, of course, goes on to tell that she lived a happy life, albeit minus a finger.

We have to admit that there is scope in this tale for the blurring of fact and fiction. The story is genuinely part of the local traditions of Chirnside. We heard it told by primary school children in the village. They learned it from a senior teacher who was born and bred in the area. There are many examples of local traditions turning out to be more accurate than versions written by partisan historians.

We were somewhat surprised to come across another story from Chirnside, this time set in the seventeenth century, well before the era of the bodysnatcher. In this a young woman is buried and comes back to life when someone tries to sever her finger. In this instance the culprit is a villainous sexton bent on robbing her of her jewellery. It seems unlikely that there were two such incidents, more likely that one story received an update a couple of centuries later.

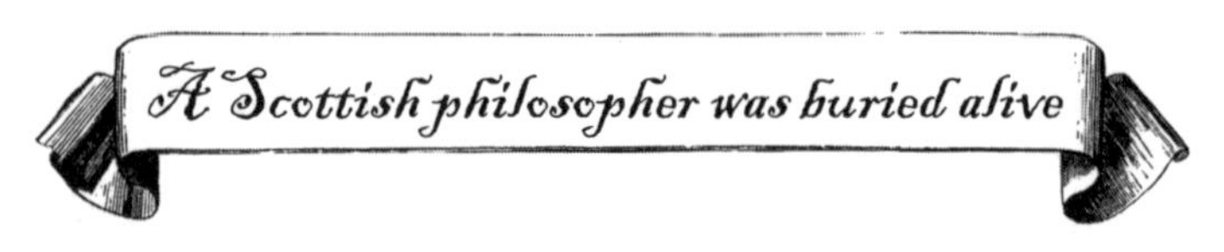

In Victorian times there was a great deal of concern about the possibility of being buried alive. Some people with a morbid fear would erect elaborate structures which would allow the awakening corpse to pull a string and ring a bell above ground. There is no doubt that it did happen. In fact it happened to one of Scotland's most brilliant philosophers.

Curiously, given the Chirnside incident, a man from nearby Duns in Berwickshire also had a catatonic incident, but with a less happy result. It was six centuries earlier. John Duns Scotus took his name from where he was born in the 1260s. He came to be regarded as one of the most important philosopher/ theologians in medieval Europe. He has the distinction of adding a word to the language: his followers, known for their intransigence, were called 'Dunses' which has come down to us as 'dunces'.

John Scotus, despite his genius, turned out to be not too bright about letting people know of his medical problems. On orders from the Franciscan Minister General, he travelled at short notice to Cologne in 1308. His servant was to follow. John took ill and, apparently, died. He was laid in a coffin and placed in a vault. His servant, who had been unavoidably delayed, was horrified and cried that they had probably buried his master alive.

The servant was aware that John suffered from fits which left him in a coma, a death-like state. He would recover after a time. The servant knew, but no one in Cologne did. When the coffin was opened they did indeed find his hands torn, his fingers shredded in a desperate attempt to get out of his tomb.

The story was recorded in Francis Bacon's *Historia Vitae et Mortis*. A Latin inscription on Duns Scotus's tomb is translated as follows:

Mark this man's demise, O traveler,
For here lies John Scot, once interr'd
But twice dead; we are now wiser
And still alive, who then so err'd.

Glasgow man galvanised

For the science of anatomy to proceed at all there had to be some legal way of obtaining corpses. There was: the bodies of hanged criminals.

In 1818, curiously the same year that Mary Shelley's *Frankenstein* was published, there were two exhibitions for the entertainment of the public in Glasgow.

The first was in Jail Square at the foot of the Saltmarket. Matthew Clydesdale, a weaver from Airdrie, was convicted for the murder of a 70-year-old man. He was sentenced to be hanged and dissected.

On 1 September he was brought to the Square. Also on the scaffold was a young thief called Simon Ross. It was the first execution in Glasgow for some time and a big crowd turned out to watch. Soldiers were deployed to keep the crowd under control. There was also a rumour that a team of Lanarkshire miners were on the way to rescue Clydesdale. They didn't materialise.

When the convicts were pronounced dead, Clydesdale was let down and placed in a cart, in which he was transported up the Saltmarket, across the Trongate and up the High Street to Glasgow University.

For the second time that day Matthew was on public display, this time for his dissection. The anatomy theatre was packed.

The anatomists were Dr Andrew Ure, senior lecturer at the recently founded Anderson's Institution and Professor James Jeffray, Professor of Anatomy, Botany & Midwifery at Glasgow University.

The story of the events did not get much attention at the time but Peter Mackenzie, a writer and 'character' of Glasgow who claimed to have been present, recounted the events in his three-volume *Reminiscences of Glasgow and the West of Scotland* in the 1860s. The proceedings had commenced when Clydesdale suddenly burst to life, shocking the entire audience. The response of the anatomist was to grab a scalpel and slit the poor man's throat, killing him for the second time that day. So much for the belief that you can't be executed twice for the same crime.

MacKenzie's account was dramatic but not entirely accurate. The reality, however, was even more bizarre – the anatomists quite deliberately intended to bring Clydesdale back to life (up to a point).

The facts are stranger than the fiction

In the 1980s Dr Fred Pattison, whose ancestor Granville Sharp Pattison was an anatomist who was tried for bodysnatching, unearthed Dr Ure's account:

> This event, however little desirable with a murderer, and perhaps contrary to the law, would yet have been pardonable in one instance, as it would have been highly honourable and useful to science.

The science behind the experiment was 'galvanisation', the use of electric stimulation. Preliminary dissection had exposed various sites on the man's body. Rods attached to a galvanic battery charged with dilute nitric and sulphuric acids were attached to Clydesdale's nervous system. The first attachment to the heel and spinal cord induced a violent kick which nearly knocked an assistant over. This might have been impressive enough, but we can only imagine the awed hush from the audience at the next step ... Clydesdale started breathing. The rods had been attached to the phrenic nerve and diaphragm. As Ure himself put it:

> The success of it was truly wonderful. Full, nay, laborious breathing instantly commenced. The chest heaved and fell; the belly was protruded and again collapsed, with the retiring and collapsing diaphragm.

Perhaps the most dramatic events occurred when the current was applied to the supraorbital nerve and heel. By varying the voltage:

> ... most horrible grimaces were exhibited ... Rage, horror, despair, anguish and ghastly smiles united their hideous expression in the murderer's face. At this period several spectators were forced to leave the apartment from terror or sickness, and one gentleman fainted.

The show was astounding but at no time did Clydesdale actually come to life, nor had the anatomists any expectation that he would. Fred Pattison does draw attention to a note of Ure's that passing current through brass knobs placed on the skin over the phrenic nerve might be effective in restoring life. He was close to describing a defibrillator.

The case of the canary

Although it lost its currency and measurements, Scotland did maintain its own separate legal system, based around the Sheriff Courts. The Glasgow sheriff was challenged by this case in the mid-nineteenth century.

Peter Mackenzie's *Reminiscences of Glasgow and the West of Scotland* proves to be a treasure house of strange but true stories. We know from the Clydesdale case that his accuracy in reporting may be flawed, but felt it worth relaying this story.

The Shanks family were living in one of the mansions in St Andrew's Square, Glasgow, having recently returned from the West Indies. They had a well-loved pet canary. The bird made a bid for freedom, flying through an open window. It alighted, in the first instance, on the steps of St Andrew's church.

In Mackenzie's words, 'This pretty, fluttering, innocent Canary bird, was soon seen and chased and caught on the steps of St. Andrew's Church, by a poor little beggar boy, soliciting alms in the neighbourhood, who treated it most kindly; he pressed it into the bosom of his tattered shirt …'

The boy's action was observed by a Mr Pinkerton, a prominent wine merchant. Since the boy would have no way of keeping the bird in the comfort it was used to, Pinkerton offered the boy 1*s* 6*d* for it. It was a good day's income for the boy and he was happy to accept. Pinkerton took the bird home, provided a cage and all the necessary accoutrements. His family called it Dicky.

The Shanks family were distressed at the loss of their pet. They had handbills printed offering a reward for the safe return of the bird.

Despite his family's attachment to Dicky, Pinkerton did the honourable thing and reported his story to the Shanks. He offered to return the bird, with the small proviso that his outlay of 1*s* 6*d* be repaid, a paltry sum to this class of people.

The Shanks did not see it that way; instead they threatened him 'that if he did not beg their pardon, and immediately restore the bird to them, they would punish him with the action of the Law'. Pinkerton was provoked by this and demanded that they prove that this was indeed their canary.

> And here a thumping law plea began, which ultimately cost some hundreds of pounds but which might have been settled at the outset for one shilling and sixpence on the head of the poor Canary; and yet that Canary deserves to be immortalised, for the wonderful results it produced in all the Courts of this kingdom of Scotland ...

The Shanks employed Mr Michael Gilfillan, a prominent lawyer who argued in a ten- or twelve-page document that Mr Pinkerton 'had stolen, or fraudulently obtained possession of their bird'.

Pinkerton employed Mr Alex Ure who contended that Pinkerton 'became the bona fide purchaser of it, in broad day-light, on the public streets of Glasgow...'.

The arguments raged on. The sheriff, a Mr Hamilton, eventually judged against Pinkerton and ordered the return of the bird. But the bird was dead, the victim of a stray cat: 'Mr. Ure, recapitulating the fact that the bird had been slain, and the cat itself hanged for the foul deed.'

So it was back to court again. The court was increasingly upset that so much of its time was being wasted over the trifling matter of 1*s* 6*d*. Mackenzie contends that it was a case that ultimately led to a change in the law in Scotland: the setting up of the Small Claims court.

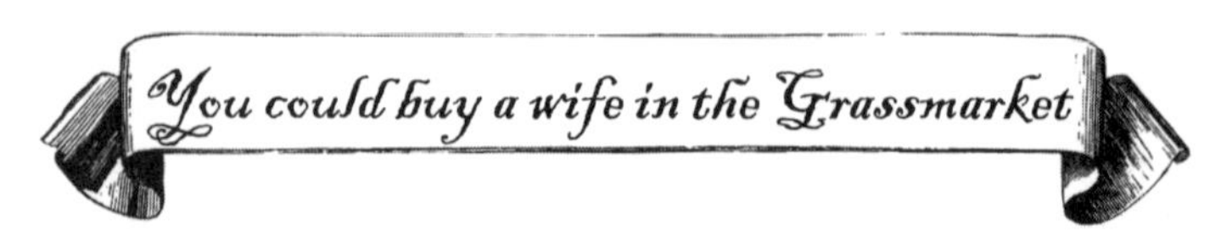

You could buy a wife in the Grassmarket

In 1828 Mary Mackintosh was put up for sale in the Grassmarket in Edinburgh. She had a straw rope tied around her middle and the words 'To be sold by public auction' around her neck. The proceedings were recorded in great detail by a broadside (broadsides were publications containing news, sold on the streets).

The event drew a big crowd. A Highland drover opened the bidding at 10 and 20*s* (£1.50). A tinker shouted that she should not be taken to the Highlands and upped the price by 6*d*. A Killarney 'pig jobber' raised by 2*s*. A brogue maker wonderfully described as being 'as drunk as fifty cats in a wallet' took exception and laid the Killarney man out before attacking the auctioneer.

A monstrous regiment of women, supposedly 700 strong, appeared, incensed by the entire proceeding. They attacked the crowd armed with stones in stockings. The auctioneer and the husband of the woman for sale were beaten as the whole scene turned into a general battle, with only the arrival of the police stopping lives being lost.

After the disturbance had been quelled bidding resumed and the lady was sold to a widowed farmer for the price of £2 5*s*.

The Orcadian headhunter

Jack Renton from Stromness followed many of his fellow Orcadians to sea. Like many, he returned with tales to tell. Jack's story was exciting enough – Shanghaied, captured by 'savages', escaping on a slave ship – but it has only recently emerged that he didn't tell the whole truth. The untold part of the adventure lived on in an oral tradition 9,000 miles away from Orkney.

In 1568 the Spanish found a group of islands east of Papua New Guinea; they named them the Solomon Islands, since such a remote and lush place would surely contain treasures equal to that of the biblical king. The islands would become a British protectorate in 1898. In the intervening years they were pretty much avoided – with good reason! The islands were populated by tribes constantly warring with each other and with any visitors from outside. The Solomons gained a reputation as a dangerous place teeming with headhunters and cannibals.

It was in 1868 that Jack Renton found himself there. He had been Shanghaied in San Francisco along with four other men. The ship was a tub called the *Reynard* which was bound for McKean's island in the Pacific. The cargo she was shipping was *guano*, bird poo. We can only imagine how bad the conditions must have been on board for the five men to believe that casting themselves adrift in an open boat in the vast Pacific ocean was a better option.

The venture was as foolhardy as it sounds. Drifting for forty days, three of the men perished. The remaining two were in pretty poor shape when they ran aground on the island of Malaita, on the dangerous coast of the Solomons. The locals, turning out a welcoming party, lived up to their billing and promptly clubbed one of the men to death. For Jack Renton fate intervened in the arrival of an armed party from a rival tribe. Jack was snatched and taken to the small offshore island of Sulufou.

There he was kept as a curiosity. Jack managed to charm the local chieftain who later adopted him as a son. With the chief's protection he survived. He learned the language and tried to teach the islanders better fishing and farming techniques. For eight years he lived in what he later described as the 'most savage place on earth'.

Jack's position was not entirely unknown. Rumours circulated that a white man was living amongst the natives on the island. A Captain MacFarlane visited on a ship called *Rose and Thistle* and tried to barter for the white man's release. He came away empty-handed.

Three years later, in 1875, a slave trading ship, the *Bobtailed Nag*, anchored off the island. Jack persuaded the islanders to let him send a message to the ship. He wrote on a piece of driftwood with charcoal, 'John Renton. Please take me off to England.' The captain, a Scot named Murray, had heard rumours further down the coast, and was willing to help. Thomas Slade, one of the crew, reported that when it was clear that Jack was leaving there was 'great lamentation and real tears' from the islanders. Jack left the island with a promise that he would return with goods that would help the tribe, and returned to a hero's welcome.

That much of the story he freely told; Jack himself published his account in the *Brisbane Courier* and *The Adventures of Jack Renton* in 1875, but on the Solomon Islands he was not forgotten. Mike McCoy, an Australian biologist, lived among the modern islanders for twenty-six years. He discovered that the history of the Malaition people retained in the oral tradition by the tribal storytellers featured a white man. The man, Jack Renton, had indeed been on the island, he had indeed assimilated into the tribal culture and that did indeed include participation in the warfare against neighbouring clans. As Mike McCoy puts it:

> There is no doubt that Renton became a headhunter. He would have had to for his street credibility. The islanders recall even now what a strong warrior he was. Renton was accepted into male society and lived in the men's long house. He apparently killed several people from inland and took heads. His warrior prowess and closeness to the salt-water people chief, Kabou, led to the bush people putting a bounty on his head. When he went to his favourite spots – one was an idyllic-looking natural swimming pool on the main island - he always had an armed guard to protect him.

These revelations make sense of the objects Jack brought home with him, a spear and a necklace of sixty-four human teeth, which are now in the National Museum of Scotland.

Jack, like Mungo Park before him, could not settle back in Scotland and did return as promised to the island, bringing tools and supplies. His knowledge of the culture and language led to him being recruited by the Queensland government to explore the area and control the activities of the slave traders.

In 1878 Jack, en route to Australia, went ashore on the *New Hebrides* with a companion to collect water. When he didn't return to the ship a search party went ashore and returned with two bodies. Two bodies, but neither was complete. The 'Great White Head Hunter' had lost his head.

Women are the best salmon catchers

It is widely known among fishermen, or should that be fisherpersons, that women are better at catching salmon than men. This is epitomised by the fact that the biggest salmon ever caught on rod and line in the British Isles was caught by Georgina Ballantine on the Glendelvine beat of the River Tay. At 64lb (29.02988kg for our younger readers), 54in long (1.3766m), it has never been beaten, nor is it ever likely to be.

Georgina is not the only lady who has beaten the men to the biggest fish: Clementina Morrison caught a 61lb salmon from the River Deveron in October 1924; Doreen Davey caught a 59½lb salmon in March 1923 from the Wye; Gladys Blanche Huntington caught a 55lb salmon from the River Awe; and Lettice Ward caught a 50lb fish from the Kinnaird beat of the Tay.

Georgina Ballantine's fish tops them all. On 7 October 1922 Georgina got a message that the laird would not be fishing on that day and that she had the opportunity to fish. 'A whole day's fishing on a glorious sunny autumn day, how I rejoiced to be alive!' she wrote in a letter recently shared by Scottish writer Bruce Sandison. In the letter she notes, 'One thing is certain, that a good deal of the angler's success – or failure – depends on the efficiency of the man on the oars. The oarsman that day was one of the finest anglers who ever cast a salmon fly on the waters of the mighty Tay – my father.'

During the course of the day she caught three fish, totalling 63lb. A good day's fishing by any standards, but then at 6.15 p.m. she hooked a fourth fish and, in her own words, after 'two hours and five minutes of nerve-wracking anxiety, thrilling excitement and good stiff work' she and her father boated the largest salmon ever caught in the British Isles.

Sandison tells:

> When a cast of Georgina's salmon was displayed in the window of PD Malloch's shop in Perth, she stood at the back of the crowd who had gathered to admire it. Two elderly men were particularly overawed by the size of the salmon and Georgina heard them talking: one said to the other, 'A woman? Nae woman ever took a fish like that oot of the water, mon. I would need a horse, a block and tackle, tae tak a fish like that oot. A woman – that's a lee anyway.'

The cast is now in Perth Museum.

It is all down to sex

According to Professor Peter Behan of Glasgow University, a neurologist, the reason women are better at catching salmon is down to sex. Most of the monster salmon are male, and human female scent is more attractive to them (a strong sense of smell is widely believed to be at least part of the reason that salmon can find their way back to the river of their birth).

Observations made through an observation window in a fish ladder suggested that if a man put a finger in the water upstream the fish would become agitated and would hang back for half an hour, while if a woman put her whole hand in the water the fish would be unperturbed. In his book *Salmon and Women – the Feminine Angle* written with Wilma Patterson, Professor Behan puts this phenomenon down to pheromones

– sex hormones. This theory has led to men tying flies with their wife's pubic hair.

In his 2012 book *Glorious Gentlemen*, Sandison asked the question of a number of Scotland's top ghillies (angling guides). Their answer was that women do make the best salmon anglers, but because they are more patient, more willing to listen to advice and less inclined to engage in the macho aim of casting to the far bank no matter where the fish are, rather than it being down to biochemistry.

The tall and short of it

In 1862 Jennie Quigley left Glasgow for America. She was 13 years old and was under 2ft tall (she did eventually reach 41in). She was taken on by P.T. Barnum, named the 'Scottish Queen' and was billed the smallest woman in the world. As a performer and actress she toured the world along with other small performers such as 'Commodore Foote' and his sister the 'Fairy Queen'. Although she never married it appears that she did have a liaison with a Commodore Nutt.

A reviewer described Quigley as 'a charming mite of femininity who captured the hearts of everybody by the perfection of the acting as well as by her personal beauty and naturalness of character'. She retired in 1917 after fifty years in showbusiness.

Angus Mor MacAskill was born in 1825 on the Isle of Berneray in the Sound of Harris. He was rated by the *Guinness Book of Records* as the tallest non-pathological giant in history, standing at 7ft 9in.

At an early age he moved with his parents to Canada as a 'normal'-sized child. It was only when he reached adolescence that he had a prodigious growth spurt. He quickly became known for his astounding strength. He could lift a ship's anchor weighing 2,800lb – over a ton. He could carry a 350lb barrel under each arm and it was claimed that he once lifted a horse over a 4ft fence.

In 1849 he started working for P.T. Barnum's show, appearing alongside the tiny 'General Tom Thumb'. He toured many parts of the world, including a requested performance in Windsor Castle for Queen Victoria. After retiring from showbusiness he settled in Englishtown in Nova Scotia where he died at the tragically young age of 37. His death came in the year before Jennie Quigley arrived in America, so the two Scottish superstars never met.

There are two museums dedicated to Angus Mor MacAskill, one in Englishtown and one, set up by Peter MacAskill, in Dunvegan on the Isle of Skye.

Lighthouses

Robert Louis Stevenson's grandfather was also Robert Stevenson. Robert Stevenson's life changed when his mother, who had been widowed young, remarried. Robert's stepfather, Thomas Smith, was an engineer. He took the boy on as an apprentice and later as a partner.

In 1791, at the age of 19, he was trusted with the supervision of the construction of a lighthouse on the island of Little Cumbrae on the Clyde, followed by a lighthouse on the Pentland Skerries. While, in a long career, he also designed roads, bridges and railway lines, lighthouses became his speciality. He designed over fifteen of them all around the coast of Scotland. Several of his innovations became standard across the world.

The lighthouse-Stevenson connection did not end there. All three of Robert's sons designed lighthouses: David was responsible for over thirty; Alan for thirteen; Thomas another thirty. David's two sons, David and Charles, added another thirty to the tally. Well over 100 in all, keeping shipping safe around the Scottish coast from Muckle Flugga to St Abbs Head, from the Butt of Lewis to Girdleness. A remarkable engineering dynasty.

Thomas's son, Robert Louis, was a huge disappointment to his family. He constructed some of the best loved literature of his age. But lighthouses? Not one!

Dr Jekyll was real

William Brodie was a Deacon of the Guild of Wrights and a member of the Town Council. He had a respectable reputation in Edinburgh. He also had five children, a mistress and a gambling problem. Keeping up appearances was expensive. He realised that his position allowed him to visit wealthy houses and case the joints. Alongside cabinet making, he also ran a locksmith business giving him access to keys to copy. He had a distinct advantage in his secondary career as a burglar!

He had three accomplices to help his night-time personality: Brown, Smith and Ainsley. His most daring raid was also his last. The target was His Majesty's Excise Office in the Cannongate – it was a disaster. Ainsley and Brown were caught. They quickly turned King's Evidence and Brodie was arrested and duly sentenced to hang.

There are two strange stories connected with the execution. One is that Brodie, a man of good standing, had himself recommended improvements to the gallows, introducing a forward-thinking drop mechanism to replace the old ladder. Tradition has it that he was the first person to feel the benefit of the new system.

The second story is that Brodie contrived to survive the hanging. The details are a bit hazy. The hangman was bribed to shorten the rope to stop his neck being broken. Brodie lodged a silver tube in his own throat to stop his windpipe being crushed, or perhaps it was an iron collar. A doctor was waiting to revive him when he was rushed from the gallows. All was to no avail and Deacon Brodie was indeed hanged to death.

A century on, R.L. Stevenson wrote the play *Deacon Brodie: A Double Life* and later took up the double-life theme in the much more successful *Strange Case of Dr Jekyll and Mr Hyde.*

Robert Louis Stevenson gave away his birthday

While in Samoa, Robert Louis learned that Annie, the young daughter of an American friend, was upset that she had been born on Christmas day. This meant that she never got a proper birthday as it was lost in the annual celebrations of that day. He had proper legal documents drawn up and witnessed, gifting his birthday on 13 November to Annie. She used that date for the rest of her life.

The architect who wasn't

When plans were made to erect a prominent monument to Sir Walter Scott, the design was to be chosen by competition. A young carpenter drew a design in just five days and won the contest.

George Meikle Kemp, who grew up in Carlops in the Borders, had no architectural training but he did have a passion for ancient buildings. He taught himself the skill of technical drawing and recorded many buildings in the Borders and later in Glasgow. His particular favourite was Melrose Abbey.

When the competition was announced he produced a design borrowing heavily from the style of Melrose Abbey. He submitted the drawings under a pseudonym. Out of fifty-four entries he came third. The committee, however, were not agreed on the final choice. The top entries were asked to revise and resubmit. George Meikle Kemp came out on top.

His vision dominates Princes Street today. Sadly, he didn't see it completed. One foggy evening he fell in the Union Canal and drowned.

There is a monument to George a few miles north of Peebles on the Edinburgh Road. It is somewhat less grand than the one he designed for Sir Walter.

Freedom!

Scotland's association with the cry 'Freedom!' does not start with a Mel Gibson movie. We have to go back nearly 700 years to the Declaration of Arbroath, 'It is in truth not for glory, nor riches, nor honours that we are fighting, but for freedom alone, which no honest man gives up but with life itself'. This noble sentiment is part of a letter sent by a committee of Scottish nobles to the Pope in 1320. The letter, signed in Arbroath Abbey, asked His Holiness to persuade Edward, or any other English king, to keep off their backs. The statement itself is an admirable one. Many Scots have stood by it, at home and across the world.

We cannot assert that Scots have universally stood for peace and equality. There is little doubt that Scottish soldiers, men and officers were essential in the establishment and maintenance of the British Empire. Little doubt that Scottish pioneers, engineers and administrators made that empire work. Little doubt that Scottish settlers were notably hard on the natives that stood in their way.

It is equally true that Scots have been at the forefront of struggles against oppression and battles for freedom across the world.

Glasgow slave streets

In 2007 there was a reappraisal of a conveniently forgotten chapter in Scottish history – its part in the slave trade. Marking the 200th anniversary of the Slave Trade Act of 1807, exhibitions, events and tours revealed that Glasgow's key industries, tobacco, sugar and cotton were inextricably linked to slave labour.

'The Slave Trade Act', passed by the British Government, only applied to the British Empire and did not in fact ban slavery. The Act banned trading in slaves. It would not be until 'The Abolition of Slavery Act' twenty-six years later that slavery would be officially ended. Nevertheless, the Royal Navy's West Africa squadron seized many slave ships and freed over 100,000 Africans. It was 1865 before the Thirteenth Amendment finally ended slavery in America.

In the early eighteenth century Glasgow established itself as the premier Scottish port in transatlantic trade. By the middle of the century Glasgow dominated the highly lucrative tobacco trade. Merchants shipped tobacco from the slave-driven plantations home, and then redistributed it throughout Europe. The wealth generated went into prestigious buildings in the city. The key players in the business are celebrated in the streets of Glasgow: William Cunninghame built a mansion which is now the Gallery of Modern Art; Glassford, Buchanan, Ingram and Oswald have streets named after them. There are also Jamaica Street, Tobago Street and the Kingston Bridge to remind us of the West India connection. Bishop Pococke, a visitor to Glasgow in 1760, remarked that, 'the city has above all others felt the advantages of the union in the West Indian trade which is very great, especially in tobacco, indigoes and sugar'.

People in Scotland were mostly at arm's length from the realities of slavery, but there were many Scots who travelled across the Atlantic and did get their hands dirty as plantation owners or as factors on the tobacco and sugar estates. By 1770 a quarter of Jamaica's population was Scottish; there were 100 Africans with the surname of MacDonald (Sir Trevor MacDonald being a descendant) and there was an equally strong contingent of Campbells. Plantation names in Jamaica included Aberdeen, Dalvey, Monymusk, Hermitage, Hampden, Glasgow, Argyle, Glen Islay, Dundee, Fort William, Montrose, Roxbro, Dumbarton, Old Monklands and Mount Stewart.

Scots were also active in the North American plantations. It is an eternal shame that Scots, in later years, were heavily involved in the Ku Klux Klan. The infamous 'Fiery Cross' was a Highland emblem.

Slavery was to come to an end but its contribution to the development of Scottish industry was important. It is positive that 2007 saw a recognition of the contribution to, and an admission of, Scotland's role in that barbaric chapter in history.

Petitions

It is strange but true that while Glasgow was benefiting from the slavery-related industries, Scots were at the forefront of the movement to have slavery abolished.

In the same year that 13,000 Glasgow residents put their name to a petition to abolish slavery, Robert Burns, who at one point planned to go to Jamaica, published the 'The Slave's Lament':

> The burden I must bear, while the cruel scourge I fear,
> In the lands ofVirginia,-ginia, O;
> And I think on friends most dear, with the bitter, bitter tear,
> And alas! I am weary, weary O:
> And I think on friends most dear, with the bitter, bitter tear,
> And alas! I am weary, weary O:

He was not alone in his concern for the Africans. Abolitionism can justifiably be described as the first human rights campaign in history. Large numbers of people were involved in protests, petitions, boycotts and the production of propaganda. Many wore badges or wristbands to show their support, and many carried the image of a kneeling slave and the slogan 'Am I not a man and a brother?'

Lots of Scots were outspoken. Many societies were formed such as The Glasgow Anti-Slavery Society, Glasgow Ladies' Emancipation Society, Glasgow New Ladies' Anti-Slavery Society and the Glasgow Emancipation Society. The Abolitionist Committee in Edinburgh was thought to be the third strongest in Britain after those of London and Manchester.

William Dickson from Moffat had worked as the Governor's Secretary in Barbados where he had seen the slave system first hand. When he returned to Scotland he campaigned relentlessly, travelling the country and encouraging the signing of petitions. All kinds of groups from all over Scotland, including churches, universities and town burghs, sent petitions to Parliament. In four years, 185 were sent.

Zachary MacAulay had also seen slavery with his own eyes in Jamaica. He became Governor of Sierra Leone, a colony set up as a refuge for ex-slaves. He took the huge risk of travelling on a slave ship to gather evidence. He wrote his notes in classical Greek to avoid detection of his motives by the crew.

Women, such the Quaker Jane Smeal, from Glasgow, and Eliza Wigham, from Edinburgh, were very active in creating a precedent for the suffragette campaigns to come.

Given that most people in Scotland had never seen an African and that the gruesome realities were far away, they were hardly aware of their countrymen's involvement. It is gratifying that today you can step off Buchanan Street into Nelson Mandela Place.

> **By the way, the first Africans were probably seen in Scotland in the ninth century. Viking ships returned from raiding Morocco, bringing black slaves back with them.**

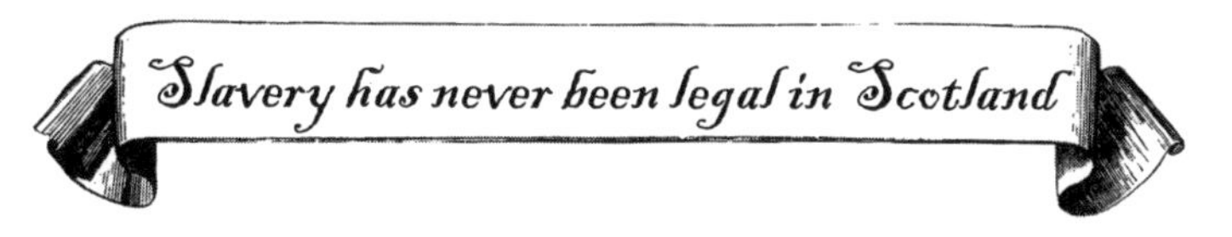

In the latter half of the eighteenth century the Court of Session in Edinburgh was asked to judge on the legality of slavery in Scotland. Two cases failed to make it to court as one or other of the protagonists died, however in 1778 the case of Knight versus Wedderburn was heard.

Joseph Knight (named after the captain of his slave ship) was captured in Guinea, West Africa, while still a child. Transported to Jamaica, he was purchased by John Wedderburn and taken to his plantation called Culloden. Wedderburn was a survivor of the battle. It seems that he took a shine to the boy and employed him as a house slave. Wedderburn later admitted that a life in the sugar fields would probably have killed him. Joseph was allowed to learn to read and write alongside his master's children and was even baptised – which was uncommon for an African at that time.

In 1769 Wedderburn returned to Scotland, settling on his estate of Ballindean in Perthshire and bringing Joseph with him. Joseph stayed with the servants and was even allowed to learn a trade as a barber. For an African he was relatively well off, but received no wages. He was still a slave.

Joseph was growing up; he began a relationship with a house servant called Annie, and when she became pregnant Wedderburn dismissed her upon which she moved to Dundee. Although the baby died, Joseph maintained the relationship and Annie fell pregnant again. He approached Wedderburn and asked for a cottage or at least wages so he could support the woman and child. Wedderburn refused and Joseph left.

Now Wedderburn turned to the court. The Justices of the Peace in Perth upheld his rights of property. Joseph was arrested and returned to Ballindean.

In 1774 Joseph Knight's lawyer, MacLaurin, appealed to the Sheriff of Perth claiming that the act of landing in Scotland freed Joseph from perpetual servitude, as slavery was not recognised in Scotland. The Sheriff found that, 'the state of slavery is not recognised by the laws of this kingdom, and is inconsistent with the principles thereof: That the regulations in Jamaica, concerning slaves, do not extend to this kingdom; and repelled the defender's claim to a perpetual service'.

Wedderburn was not satisfied and took the case to the Court of Session in Edinburgh. He argued that, even though Knight was not recognised as a slave, he was still bound to provide perpetual service in the same manner as an indentured servant or an apprenticed artisan. Joseph delivered a forty-page address (some of it in French) dealing with his life from his enslavement in Africa, through the horrors of the plantations, to his new family in Scotland.

Lord Auchinleck (father of James Boswell), one of the judges on the panel, said, 'Although in the plantations they have laid hold of the poor blacks, and made slaves of them, yet I do not think that is agreeable to humanity, not to say to our Christian religion. Is a man a slave because he is black? No. He is our brother; and he is a man, although not of our colour; he is in a land of liberty, with his wife and child, let him remain there.'

The court ruled that, 'the Dominion assumed over this Negro, under the law of Jamaica, being unjust, could not be supported in this country to any extent: That, therefore, the defender had no right to the Negro's service for any space of time, nor to send him out of the country against his consent: That the Negro was likewise protected under the act 1701, from being sent out of the country against his consent.'

It was thus confirmed in Scottish Law that slavery was not and had never been legal in Scotland and that any slave could get protection from the court if they chose to leave service or were being forced to leave the country. Joseph's life was fictionalised by James Robertson in the 2004 book *Joseph Knight*.

Certainly Scots have supported freedom causes by military means; Admiral Cochrane's stature as a national hero in Peru, Chile and Greece are an example, as we have seen. Scots have also proved themselves as relentless and effective campaigners.

Africa's first freedom fighter

David Livingstone from Blantyre was known to many Africans as 'the first African freedom fighter'. This was due to his tireless campaigning against slavery.

Unlike many other explorers, Livingstone did not have the benefit of a wealthy background to support his activities. Livingstone's family had left the Hebrides in search of work and settled in Blantyre. Living in a tenement, they eked out a living. He recalls in the introduction to *Missionary Travels and Researches in South Africa*, 'The earliest recollection of my mother recalls a picture so often seen among the Scottish poor — that of the anxious housewife striving to make both ends meet. At the age of ten I was put into the factory [Blantyre Cotton Works] as a 'piecer' to aid by my earnings in lessening her anxiety'. In the same passage he reveals the determination that was to see him become one of the most famous Scots of his generation, 'With a part of my first week's wages I purchased Ruddiman's *Rudiments of Latin*.'

His father, a staunch Presbyterian, was suspicious of the books of science and other subjects, feeling that his son should only be reading authorised books on theology. David's search for self-education was relentless. In 1836 he was admitted to Anderson's College in Glasgow, now the University of Strathclyde. He studied medicine alongside divinity with the intention of becoming a medical missionary. In due course he was accepted by the London Missionary Society for further training.

David Livingstone's African adventures were the result of a chance meeting

China was his initial goal, but a meeting with Robert Moffat, who was on leave from a mission in South Africa, convinced him otherwise. He made his way to Africa and found himself in 'Bakwain country', Bechuanaland. It is typical of the man that he cut himself off from all European contacts for months so as to better learn the language and customs of the natives.

David Livingstone was saved by a tartan jacket

In his book, Livingstone recounts in detail how a tartan jacket saved his life. A pride of lions had been taking livestock. The natives, fearing the lions were bewitched, were reluctant to tackle the animals. Livingstone led a hunting party into the field. He fired both barrels into a lion, but while he was reloading, the lion, in 'his paroxysm of dying rage', leapt, catching him on the shoulder then pinning him to the ground with its paw on his head. A second man distracted the lion and was also injured. The animal injured a third man before falling dead. Livingstone's shoulder wound left him with a partly disabled arm, but it was fortunate that it did not become infected. He put this down to the tartan jacket he was wearing, believing that it had cleaned the virus from the lion's teeth as they penetrated.

A Scottish name lives on

After a brief return to Scotland (he stayed in Hamilton) Livingstone was back in Africa. He was taken to a holy site known as Mosi-oa-Tunya ('the smoke that thunders'). He was the first European to see it:

> The most wonderful sight I had seen in Africa ... In looking down into the fissure one sees nothing but a dense white cloud which ... had two rainbows in it. From this cloud rushed up a great jet of vapour, exactly like steam ... condensing, it changed its hue to that of dark smoke and came back in a constant shower which wetted us to the skin.

He named the spectacular waterfall Victoria Falls. He points out that this was the only feature in Africa to which he gave an English name.

He did also leave behind the name of the town, Blantyre, in Malawi. It is a huge mark of the esteem he holds to this day that the name has not been changed in the way most other colonial place names have – likewise the fact that his statue still stands proud, by Mosi-ao-Tunya (formerly Victoria Falls), in the black African country of Zimbabwe. Stranger still is that when its removal was proposed in 2003, the proposal was by another black African state, Zambia, who wanted it erected on their side of the river. David Livingstone's reputation remains powerful.

Missionary Travels and Researches in South Africa

From 1854 to 1856 Livingstone crossed the width of Africa, west to east, reaching the coast in Mozambique. No one had achieved the journey at that latitude. Unlike other expeditions which took small armies of armed guards and porters, Livingstone travelled light, with just a few Africans, and bartered for supplies along the way.

He became convinced that a proper exploration of the Zambezi was vital and returned to Britain to gather support and publish *Missionary Travels and Researches in South Africa*. The Zambezi expedition was riddled with problems from the start with trouble among the crew. They encountered unknown impassable rapids and had to abandon their boat. It was widely judged a failure, causing some decline in popularity at home and making it difficult to raise funds. However, he did set out in 1866 from Zanzibar to find the source of the Nile. He thought he had found a potential candidate in the River Lualaba, but consequently discovered that it ultimately flowed west into the Congo Basin.

By 1869 he was in bad shape. Overcome by disease he was rescued by Arab slave traders, but then kept for a time caged as a public spectacle. By 1871 he was reduced to writing his journal on a newspaper over the newsprint using ink he concocted from local berries. The journal survives and in it he records a horrendous massacre, which deeply affected him: '… two guns were fired and a general flight took place – firing on the helpless canoes took place – a long line heads oh heads in the water shewed the number that would perish – great numbers died – it was awful – terrible - a dreadful world this'.

'Dr Livingstone, I presume?'

Later that year Henry Morton Stanley of the *New York Herald* eventually found Livingstone and uttered the immortal words, 'Dr Livingstone, I presume?', or perhaps he didn't. The line was included in the editorial of the *New York Herald* and has been quoted faithfully in many publications since, but curiously the relevant page of Stanley's diary was torn out.

Livingstone finally succumbed to disease in 1873 at the age of 60. His body was transported back to Britain and he was laid to rest in Westminster Abbey. In a curious echo of Robert the Bruce, his heart was buried in his beloved Africa.

It is incredible that a Scotsman born into a working-class family should be laid to rest in Westminster Abbey, have statues in Edinburgh and Zambia and have a dedicated museum in his home town of Blantyre. It is especially incredible when you consider that both his Zambezi and Nile expeditions were failures and that in his role as a missionary it is said that he only converted one African to Christianity (a chief named Sechele, though even he was reluctant to give up his five wives).

It is perhaps for his unflinching opposition to the slave trade that he is best remembered. He provided vital first-hand evidence of the atrocities being committed in Africa, fuelling the abolitionist campaigns at home. In his 1871 journal he recounts many incidents of slaves, slave traders and slave captures – six years after slavery was officially abolished in America.

He never lost his love of Africa and its people. Shortly before his death he wrote of, 'The glorious tropical vegetation in all its richness, beauty and majestic forms … beasts, lakes and rivers, and humanity in endless variety and of beautiful form.'

A Cherokee Chief

In general our view of Native Americans comes from Western movies and is appallingly flawed. In particular we have little understanding of the difference between the nations. Mention Cherokee and we are likely to think of a generic horse riding, tepee-living Indian with mesas and buttes in the background. This is far from the truth. When they were first encountered by Europeans, they were settled farmers and herdsmen living in what we would think of as the Deep South, east of the Mississippi.

The land was coveted by the white settlers and in 1829 the state of Georgia parcelled up the Cherokee territory on a map and sold lottery tickets to white settlers. The prizes were these plots, despite the fact that the natives were still living on their cherished land. Conflict ensued leading to the infamous 'Trail of Tears' when the nation was forced to march to Arkansas, thousands of them dying along the way.

Their Principal Chief for much of this complicated period fought the white man not on the battlefield, but in the courts. He was dressed not in buckskin and beads, but much as we would expect any Victorian gentleman. His name was George Ross and he was Scottish. His father was from Sutherland, and his mother's father from Inverness. Only his maternal great-grandmother was Cherokee. Most of the whites working and trading with the natives were Scots, mostly Highlanders.

While his first wife's influence may have helped (Quatie Brown Henley was well-connected in the tribe), it was because of his strength of character and his personal abilities that John Ross rose to such prominence. He was called by some the Moses of his people. He fought tirelessly to stop the Cherokee from splitting up and being removed from their homeland. He was ultimately unsuccessful. The march of American 'civilisation' was unstoppable.

George Rosie personally explored John Ross's story, recounted in his book *Curious Scotland*. He met with another John Ross, current chief of a Cherokee organisation, who told him:

> John Ross was our greatest chief. Without him the Cherokee would have been scattered to the winds, the way that other tribes were. He fought for the Nation longer and harder than anyone ... He was our great man. The Cherokee Nation, as we know it now, is John Ross's creation.

John Ross lived, for a time, in a two-storey mansion called Rose Cottage. It was burned to the ground during the conflicts.

Scottish surnames are common amongst Native Americans

James Hunter's book *Glencoe and the Indians* explains in detail the role of Scots in the early exploration of North America. Scots, particularly Highlanders, were more comfortable than most at heading off alone into what was thought of as the 'wilderness' and more comfortable than most at respecting the natives.

Working as trappers and traders it became common, even acceptable, for Scots to take a native wife. There were no white women within hundreds of miles. As the years progressed, with white women still in short supply, it was perfectly acceptable for a white man to marry a daughter of these mixed marriages. For a half-breed son there was no such social acceptance. For any of them to marry a European lady was unthinkable. The only option was to return to their mother's nation where they were more welcome, taking their surname with them – hence the many Rosses, MacDonalds and MacIntoshes in the nations.

A Scot in India

Allan Octavian Hume of the Home/Hume family in the Borders was the 'Father of Indian Ornithology'. He published several books, established the journal *Stray Feathers* and amassed a huge collection of bird skins and eggs which were later donated to the British Natural History Museum. There were 82,000 specimens. He was devastated when he lost a huge part of his manuscripts ('several hundredweights' by his own description). They were stolen by a servant during his absence and sold as wastepaper.

His place in ornithology is secure. His part in Indian politics was more controversial. He came to India in 1849 at the age of 20 to serve in the British administration. Over a long career he served as a district officer, head of a central department and secretary to the government. He fought with distinction in the Indian Rebellion in 1857. Afterwards, through his tact and understanding, he was able to achieve peace in the region far quicker than elsewhere in the country.

Throughout his career he campaigned for agricultural and economic improvement. His sound ideas and enthusiasm were recognised at first and he was appointed as Secretary for Commerce, Agriculture & Revenue. He was not slow at pointing out where the problems lay, repeatedly criticising government policies. In the preface to his *Agricultural Reform in India* he wrote, 'It is undeniable that in the tenures we have created, and the systems we have adopted, there have been grave errors'. He went so far as to claim that British land revenue policies were responsible for poverty in India. Not surprisingly, he lost his job.

He continued to campaign: 'there was always a hope, that amid the vicissitudes to which public affairs are subject, some lucky turn of the wheel might bring more enlightened ideas on these subjects into vogue ...'.

By 1872 he saw little hope of more enlightened thinking. He wrote in a letter, 'studied and invariable disregard, if not actually contempt for the opinions and feelings of our subjects, is at the present day the leading characteristic of our government in every branch of the administration'.

His vision was that if a committee of educated Indians were to develop a clearly thought-out strategy then they could ultimately bring peaceful change to the country. He wrote an open letter to the graduates of the University of Calcutta seeking volunteers and opened the road that led to the formation of the Indian National Congress (he served as its first secretary), and ultimately to Indian independence.

Colin Cameron

Colin Cameron from Lanark moved to Nyasaland in 1957. As a lawyer he defended Africans who were detained under a state of emergency, and joined the African National Congress. In a stand against apartheid, he stood for election in 1961 at the request of Hastings K. Banda. He served as a minister throughout the transfer of British protectorate, Nyasaland, to the independent state of Malawi. When he became aware that Banda's regime was becoming oppressive, he was forced to leave the country. He continued to support refugees and the cause of a just African freedom.

A lassie from Kilmarnock

Nelson Mandela called Eleanor Kasrils from Kilmarnock 'that genteel and elegant Scottish woman'. She was a quiet soul working in a bookshop in Durban in South Africa when the Sharpville massacre occurred in which sixty-nine anti-apartheid demonstrators were killed. Stunned and disgusted, she joined the Congress of Democrats, which was aligned to the African National Congress, and was one of the first women recruited into the 'Umkhonto we Sizwe – Spear of the Nation'.

'A Dangerous Master'

Historian Christian Lous Lange said that 'Technology is a useful servant and a dangerous master'. Technology certainly has taken over our lives. Since the start of the twentieth century the pace of change has accelerated until the story of one of Scotland's greatest icons, the Loch Ness Monster, has been invaded by Internet technology.

Our favourite description of a computer was given by a young girl who described it as a 'sort of television that Daddy swears at'. In our experience they require a lot of swearing, not just when they fail to co-operate, but also when they invade our privacy and presume to tell us where we want to go, what we want to eat, what we want to wear. Yet without e-mails, search engines, online archives and even online bookshops, how would we manage?

Perhaps the single most invasive and persuasive invention of all is the television. Every evening 20 million people in the UK sit down to watch telly. It's hard to imagine life without it. A generation has grown up with it as a daily companion. In a project which explored the deprivation suffered by children throughout the twentieth century, including two wars, the revelation that shocked twenty-first century-school kids more than any other was that in the past you had to get up out of your seat and walk across the room and turn a knob to change channels on the television.

The invention was, of course, Scottish.

John Logie Baird

It is well known that the television was invented by Scotsman John Logie Baird from Helensburgh. It was not his only invention or business venture. He had a varied and often strange early career. This included a project which smacks of medieval alchemy.

He hated school. His interest in science and technology was already showing itself at an early age. While at school he took an early leap into aviation, a subject still in its infancy. He constructed a glider. When it was launched accidentally while he was working on it, it flew about as well as the Birdman of Stirling. He left flight to the Wright Brothers.

He tried to brighten the family home in Helensburgh by installing electricity, the only house in the town to have the technology. The system was somewhat temperamental and needed constant monitoring. One evening the system blacked out when his father was halfway down the stairs. He tumbled to the bottom. The power had to go.

If it was not to be power supply, what about communication? He built a telephone network extending to nearby friends. The telephone wires did not have telegraph posts to support them so he improvised by stringing the wires between nearby trees. On a dark and stormy night the wires were jostled from the branches. The sagging cable swept the driver of a horse-drawn cab off his vehicle. The telecommunication empire was over before it started.

In 1903 he made himself unpopular by experimenting with selenium, which stank the house out. His selenium cell was, however, a first step towards television. By 1912, while at the Royal Technical College in Glasgow (now the University of Strathclyde), he had seriously begun experimenting with this technology.

In 1916 he was declared unfit for military service, but was aware of the appalling conditions in the trenches. He set out to provide at least one area of comfort for the troops and created the 'Baird Undersock Company'. His socks, treated with Borax, were intended to combat the constant problem of foot infection at the front. He was himself a sufferer of cold feet (as am I). He used innovative sales techniques, employing sandwich board women (rather than men) for the first time. He also sent friends to ask for Baird Undersocks in shops which he knew didn't stock them.

Around 1918 he was working for the Clyde Valley Electrical Power Company and came up with a plan that recalls the Philosopher's Stone: the Holy Grail for medieval alchemists – the power to turn base metal into gold. Baird's plan was to turn dust into diamonds. The scheme would require electricity – a lot of it.

In his own words, from his autobiography *Sermons, Soap and Television*:

> Diamonds are created in nature by subjecting carbon to a very high pressure and a very high temperature. I thought I might get these conditions artificially by electrically exploding a rod of carbon embedded in concrete. I ... embedded the whole thing in a large iron pot. My idea was to pass a stupendous sudden current through the carbon so as to generate enormous heat and pressure. I chose a good time and then, when no-one was about, closed the switch. There was a dull thud from the pot, a cloud of smoke, and then the main current breaker tripped and the whole of the power supply went off ... I forgot about the pot and it disappeared. Perhaps it is today lying in some forgotten rubbish heap, a pot of cement with priceless diamonds embedded in it.'

He had blacked out half of Glasgow!

> **By the way, his scheme is not as crazy as it sounds and he was not the only person working on diamond manufacture, but it was not until 1953 that this was reliably achieved.**

From socks to jam

Having actually made some money from the socks, he took himself to Trinidad to start a new venture. In hardly a logical step from making socks he started making jam. He failed to take into account the local wildlife:

> Sweet smelling clouds of vapour rose from the pot and floated into the jungle. They acted like a trumpet call to the insect life and a mass of insects of all shapes and sizes appeared out of the bush in terrifying numbers. They flew into the steam above the cauldron in their thousands and, scorched, fell lifeless into the boiling jam. I dropped my stirrer and ran …

By 1920 he was back in London; the jam wasn't selling well so he took the next logical step – soap.

It was very cheap at 18*s* per hundredweight, but it was also very poor. There were complaints.

In *Sermons, Soap and Television* Baird tells the story:

> One day a very vulgar and ferociously angry woman banged her way into the office. She carried a small infant, pulled its clothes over its head and thrust a raw and inflamed posterior into my face. The poor child looked like a boiled lobster. The wretched woman had washed the infant in a strong solution of Baird's Speedy Cleaner. I calmed her down and pointed out that the Speedy Cleaner was a powerful scouring soap for floors and ship decks, and not a toilet soap for infants.

Further ventures followed, including glass razor blades and pneumatic shoes. The pneumatic shoes involved taking fellow

Scots inventor Robert Thomson's tyre idea to a new level. He inserted balloons into large boots, but on his first experimental stroll or, more accurately, a 'succession of drunken and uncontrollable lurches', one of his balloons burst, to the amusement of local urchins who had been following him.

He finally decided to concentrate on television and started making some progress, though he nearly electrocuted himself in the process. His attempts to convince others of the importance of his work did not always go well.

An attempt to convince a *Daily Express* editor ended in the man leaving the room and sending in a burly assistant. Apparently the conversation had gone, 'For God's sake, Jackson, go down to the reception room and get rid of a lunatic who is there. He says he's got a machine for seeing by wireless. Watch him carefully, he may have a razor hidden.'

Baird persevered. By 1924 he managed to transmit a flickering image across a few feet. On 26 January 1926 he gave the world's first demonstration of true television before fifty scientists in an attic room in central London. In 1927 his television was demonstrated over 438 miles of telephone line between London and Glasgow, and he formed the Baird Television Development Company. In 1928 the company achieved the first transatlantic television transmission between London and New York and the first transmission to a ship in the mid-Atlantic. He also gave the first demonstration of both colour and stereoscopic television.

Inventor and businessman John Logie Baird had finally made his mark.

A naval disaster

Sometimes the technology is flawed. In January 1918 an incident took place in the Firth of Forth which came to be known (in spite of attempts to keep the whole thing secret) as the Battle of the May Isle. This is a misnomer. No enemy vessels, equipment or personnel were involved. Not a shot was fired. It was not a battle; it was a fiasco.

Naval command decided to carry out an operation called 'ECI' involving two separate flotillas sailing out from Rosyth in Fife. The operation included battleships, cruisers and destroyers as well as nine K-class submarines.

Submarines were a relatively new concept and their capabilities and their role in warfare were still being explored. The automotive torpedo, designed by the Scot Robert Whitehead, was not yet in operation. The K-class was steam-powered (they had to be big, 320ft, to accommodate boilers and stocks of coal). They were notoriously complicated and difficult to handle. Six out of eighteen foundered in accidents and only one ever made contact with the enemy. They were nicknamed Kalamity class.

Because of potential German U-boat activity, the whole fleet were to sail without lights and to maintain radio silence. Then the fog came down.

The first flotilla was at sea, east of the Isle of May, followed by the subs. K11 spotted several small minesweepers coming out of Anstruther and turned to port, as did K17. K14 didn't realise what was happening until the last minute, and the captain engaged full rudder to avoid a collision. The rudder jammed, so the sub just kept on turning, taking him straight into the path of K22, which was going full ahead. K22 slammed straight into K14. The two vessels were stuck together and immobile, still right in the path of oncoming vessels.

Orders were forgotten, lights switched on and radio pleas for help broadcast. Three battlecruisers sailed safely past, but HMS *Inflexible* struck K22, riding over her, pushing her under, causing considerable damage.

The Mayday (m'aidez) was picked up. Some boats in the first flotilla turned to give assistance, putting them on a collision course with the second flotilla. The captain of the leading ship of the second group, reckoning he was clear of the wrecked submarines, sped up, unaware of the returning vessels. The two fleets met head on. HMS *Fearless* sliced into K17. She sank within eight minutes.

K3 and K4 turned to pick up survivors. K12 turned back to help, narrowly missing a cruiser. Her unexpected appearance caused K6, newly arrived on the scene, to swerve to avoid a collision, resulting in driving straight into K4, almost cutting her in half. K4 went down with no survivors.

K7 was now picking up survivors but wash from the oncoming ships swept survivors and rescuers into the water. Many men in the water were driven under by the second flotilla speeding over them.

The operation ended with over 100 lives lost. Two K-class subs were lost and three more were badly damaged. The inadequacies of the design were spectacularly and tragically demonstrated. Astoundingly the navy went on to order six more of them, although, with the end of the war, only one was ever completed.

The Glasgow vampire

The Southern Necropolis in Glasgow is a spooky enough place, but imagine what it was like for police officer Alex Deeprose when, in 1954, he turned up to investigate a disturbance in the graveyard. The place was filled with children armed with bread knives and sharpened sticks. They were searching for a vampire!

The vampire, so the rumour had gone, was 7ft tall and had iron teeth for the shredding of small children. He had consumed two already!

The local children, inflamed by the story, had taken it upon themselves to seek out the monster. However, it is said that when a figure, backlit by the red light and smoke from the nearby steelworks, did appear, the children scattered.

In spite of assurances by the police and the local headmaster that no children had been reported missing in the previous months, the young 'Van Helsings' continued to turn up at dark for several nights, still seeking the 'Iron Man'. When the story was reported in the newspapers adults started to turn up as well, seeking a glimpse of the gory creature.

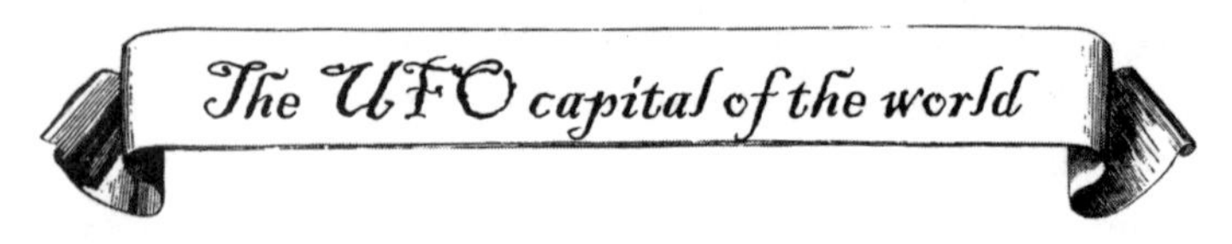

The UFO capital of the world

UFO sightings in the small town of Bonnybridge and the surrounding area, stretching from Stirling to the outskirts of Edinburgh and known as the Falkirk Triangle, are a fairly recent phenomena. They are, however, numerous, totalling around 300 sightings annually. Local councillor Billy Buchanan claims that nearly half the residents of the town have seen a UFO.

It all started in 1992 when James Walker noticed some strange lights in the sky while driving home. At first he thought they were stars but was startled when he saw them move and assume a triangle shape. More sightings quickly followed. When councillor Buchanan publicly broadcast the story to a media fanfare, the number of reports accelerated. The councillor contacted the government and, particularly, the Ministry of Defence, asking for an investigation. Could there be a rational explanation for all this activity? No answers have been forthcoming.

Most of the sightings happen at night and generally consist of lights in the sky which change shape, colour and brightness, or of several lights in formation. In recent years more and more of the sightings have been caught on video. Numerous examples can be viewed on You Tube, so you can judge for yourself.

There are plans to take advantage of the area's extra-terrestrials in attracting visitors to the town. A UFO tourist information centre is being discussed and there are discussions underway which may lead to Bonnybridge twinning with Roswell in New Mexico – the site of a famous alien landing in 1947. Roswell is quiet UFO-wise these days, but Bonnybridge is buzzing.

The Livingston encounter

While Bonnybridge's UFO activity started in 1992, we can go back to 1979 to find an astounding series of events. In Livingston, not far as the spaceship flies, an alien encounter was the subject of a police investigation.

Bob Taylor, a forest worker, returned from walking his dog on nearby Dechmont Law. He looked like he had been beaten up. He was dishevelled, his clothes torn, and he had grazes to his chin and thighs. The police agreed that an assault had taken place and set out to pursue the matter. The strange thing is that Taylor claimed he'd encountered a 'flying dome' which tried to pull him aboard. This is the only time a police force has investigated an attempted alien abduction.

Taylor claimed the 'flying dome' had been hovering in a forest clearing. The dome was about 20ft in diameter and 'a dark metallic material with a rough texture like sandpaper', and was 'set with small propellers'. Smaller spheres, similar to sea mines, grabbed him and started hauling him towards the main craft. He passed out and when he awoke they were gone. His car wouldn't start so he walked home.

Police accompanied Taylor to the site where he claimed he received his injuries. They found 'ladder-shaped marks' in the ground where Taylor said he saw the large spherical object and other marks that Taylor said were made by the smaller, mine-like objects.

Needless to say, UFO enthusiasts were delighted with the incident and happy to go along with Taylor's story. Malcolm Robinson, a founder member of Strange Phenomena Investigations (SPI) to this day believes it could be one of the few genuine cases of a UFO encounter. He said, 'About 95 per cent of UFO sightings have a natural solution but it's the 5 per cent minority that we are trying to provide answers for'. Robinson was among the first on the scene: 'I was there the following day. I saw the marks and I met Bob, who struck me as a very sane and rational gentleman who didn't want any of the publicity he had been thrust into. He never changed his story.'

The incident was re-examined in 2012 in the documentary 'UFOs – the Untold Story', made for the National Geographic Channel. UFO sceptics remain sceptical. No one was charged with the offence, however the police file is not closed.

Nessie disappeared in 2013

In 2013 the press reported that the Loch Ness Monster had disappeared. In the *Inverness Courier*, Gary Campbell, Registrar of Sightings for the Official Loch Ness Monster Club, said, 'It's very upsetting news and we don't know where she's gone. The number of sightings has been reducing since the turn of the century but this is the first time in almost 90 years that Nessie wasn't seen at all'. Mr Campbell revealed that there had been no reports for eighteen months.

Three potential sightings were dismissed as images of a wave, a duck and a picture not even taken on Loch Ness. Bookmaker William Hill accordingly failed to pay out the £1,000 prize for the best Nessie sighting for 2013.

So what had happened to the beloved beast? Predictably, global warming has been blamed. In 2008, veteran Nessie hunter Robert Rines of the US-based 'Academy of Applied Science' stated that global warming was affecting Nessie's habitat and could kill her off. Rines took the famous 'flipper' photo of Nessie in the early 1970s.

Steve Feltham, who has watched the loch for twenty-four years, reported in *The Mirror* that he has finally come to the conclusion that Nessie is not an ancient plesiosaur, but a catfish. Wels catfish introduced into Spanish rivers have grown to monstrous sizes, up to 13ft, and could be mistaken for the sinuous neck of a monster. These fish were introduced into a few British waters in Victorian times. If, as Mr Feltham suggests, they were put in the loch at the end of the nineteenth century, it would explain why modern monster sightings started in the 1930s. It would have taken that time for the catfish to reach a sufficiently monstrous size. If the population was not breeding successfully the population would now be dying out. Perhaps only one or two are left.

Most bizarrely, *The Scotsman* reported that Kevin Carlyon had taken personal responsibility for Nessie's disappearance. Mr Carlyon is the 'High Priest of White Witches' in the UK. He said, 'I personally believe Nessie is the ghost of a dinosaur, who has been regularly seen on the loch. But the spirit of the creature has been so exploited in recent years I decided to carry out an exorcism, hence no sightings of the monster'. Fortunately he did promise to return in 2014 and reverse the spell.

Ironically 2013 was the 80th anniversary of the first modern-day sighting of Nessie. She had been spotted by fishermen a few years earlier, but it was the 1933 sighting by Mr and Mrs MacKay of Drumnadrochit, reported in the *Inverness Courier*, that really kicked off Nessiemania. Between the sightings by St Columba in the sixth century and those by the McKays in the twentieth, Nessie was fairly quiet.

Since the 1930s the monster has been spotted over 1,000 times and photographed many times. Dr Robert Wilson's 1934 snap effectively became the model for Nessie and all the millions of pounds worth of pictures, models and cuddly toys which have been sold to tourists. It took the good doctor sixty years to admit that he had faked the picture with a toy from Woolworths.

Nowadays most people have a camera on their phones with them at all times, so when she does put in an appearance there is a better chance than ever of getting a picture.

Rumours of Nessie's death have been greatly exaggerated

In 2014 technology did indeed come to the aid of the Nessie mystery. A strange object was spotted on an image of Loch Ness taken by satellite and published on Apple's Map App. Zooming in on the image appears to show a giant catfish-like creature swimming just below the surface. An array of debunkers protested that the image was simply a boat and the

wake pattern it was making. There were even suggestions that the image had been digitally tampered with.

Spurred by the Apple discovery, Bjarne Sjöstrand of Stockholm searched Google Earth and located a similarly vague image. Incredibly, it won him the 2014 William Hill prize.

In 2015, not to be outdone by Apple, Google took the mapping of Loch Ness to a new level. They brought their technology to the loch and recorded it intensively. They have transformed their 'Street View' facility to a 'Loch View', both above and below the surface. There is even a little Nessie icon to guide visitors around – a whole new way to explore the largest body of freshwater in Scotland, containing more water than all the lakes in England and Wales combined.

In addition to the IT companies' input there were three sightings in 2014, and, up to the time of writing, four in 2015.

So does the Loch Ness Monster exist? As to the existence of a living breathing animal we'd rather not comment, but we can assure you that the Nessie legend, the Nessie mystery and the Nessie industry (worth £25 million per year) are all alive and well.

So we end with an old story (not the oldest, but at 1,400 years, pretty old) which is still evolving and growing today. Likewise Scottish history is growing and evolving (the big question being the future of our union with England). That evolution depends on everything that has happened in the past. How can we know where we're going if we don't know where we've been?

All this book claims to present are 'tasters' from the huge length and breadth of Scottish history. There is so much more to all of it. If any of the stories inspire the reader to delve a bit deeper and discover a little more then we will have done our job.

Recommended Reading

We have thoroughly enjoyed researching this book, delving deeper into stories we half knew and unearthing new ones. We are happy to recommend a selection of titles below. Some, such as George Rosie's *Curious Scotland*, cover a range of stories in greater detail than we have. Some explore themes, such as Billy Kay's personal journey through the activities of Scots abroad. Some pursue individual stories in great depth.

We have been hugely aided by the practise of digitising old and out-of-print publications and making these freely available online. This allows access to a wide range of books which were previously rare and expensive, such as the writings of David Livingstone and Mungo Park. We have found www.archive.org and the National Library of Scotland website particularly helpful.

The Internet has proved an endless treasure trove and we have visited too many sites to mention. Fire up your search engine and find out for yourself. While much information needs to be treated with suspicion, one thing leads to another and confirmation (or not) discovered.

There is no excuse in this age of accessible information for what Stephen Fry has termed 'in-curiosity' – a lack of interest in exploring the world around us.

Explore! Enjoy!

Baird, J.L., *Sermons, Soap and Television* (1941)
Bathhurst, B., *The Lighthouse Stevensons* (HarperCollins, 1999)
Behan, P. and Patterson, W., *Salmon and Women – the Feminine Angle* (Cassels Illustrated, 1990)

Campbell, E., Were the Scots Irish? (Antiquity, 75 [288], 2001)
Edwards, O.D., *Burke and Hare* (Polygon Books, 1980)
Foster, A., *Foster's Scottish Oddities* (Black and White Publishing, 1988)
Hamilton I.R., *Stone of Destiny* (Birlinn Ltd, 2008)
Hill, G., *An Historical Account of The MacDonnells of Antrim* (Archer & Sons, 1873)
Hume, A.O., *Agricultural Reform in India* (W.H. Allen & Co., London, 1879)
Hunter, J., *Glencoe and the Indians* (Mainstream Publishing, 1996)
Kay, B., *The Scottish World: A Journey into the Scottish Diaspora* (Mainstream Publishing, 2008)
Keay J. & J., *Collins Encyclopedia of Scotland* (HarperCollins, 1994)
Kemp, K., Back to the Wild (*New Scientist* No.3024, 2015)
Livingstone, D., *Travels and Researches in South Africa* (John Murray, London, 1857)
Mackenzie, P., *Reminiscences of Glasgow and the West of Scotland* (John Tweed, Glasgow, 1865)
Marsden, J., *Somerled* (John Donald Press, 1999)
Mawer, A., *The Vikings* (Cambridge University Press, 1913)
Maxwell Stewart, F., *Lady Nithsdale and the Jacobites* (Traquair House, 1999)
Moffat, A., *Arthur and the Lost Kingdoms* (Birlinn Ltd, 2012
Moffat, A., *The Sea Kingdoms: The History of Celtic Britain and Ireland* (Birlinn Ltd, 2008)
Noble, S., 'John Logie Baird: a Life' (notes for Helensburgh Heritage, 2007)
Parke, M., *Travels in the Interior of Africa* (Samuel Bradford, 1803)
Randell, N., *The White Headhunter: The Story of a 19th-Century Sailor Who Survived a South Seas Heart of Darkness* (Constable, 2003)

Rosie, G., *Curious Scotland, Scotland's Hidden History* (Granta Books, 2004)
Sandison, B., *Glorious Gentlemen* (Black and White Publishing, 2012)
Tranter, N., Tales *and Traditions of Scottish Castles* (Neil Wilson publishing, 1996)

If you enjoyed this book, you may also be interested in…

Aberdeen in 100 Dates

15th August 1903 - On this day Aberdeen FC played its first match, holding Stenhousemuir to a 1-1 draw. 21st April 1943 - Luftwaffe bombers dropped 130 bombs on Aberdeen, killing ninety-seven civilians and twenty-seven soldiers. 15th August 1963 - Henry John Burnett was hanged at Craiginches Prison – the last execution to take place in Scotland. Experience 100 key dates that shaped Aberdeen's history, highlighted its people's genius (or silliness) and embraced the unexpected. Featuring a mix of pivotal, social, criminal and sporting events, this book reveals a past that will fascinate, delight and even shock both residents and visitors to this Scottish city.

ISBN 978 0 7509 6031 1

Scottish Borders Folk Tales

This lively acollection of folk tales from the Scottish Borders is rich in stories both tall and true, ancient and more recent, dark and funny, fantastical and powerful. Here you will find the Lochmaben Harper, Tam Linn, Thomas the Rhymer, Muckle Mou'd Meg and Michael Scot the wizard. These well-loved and magical stories are retold in an engaging style, shaped by James Spence's many years of storytelling. Richly illustrated and enlivened by the rhythmic Scots language of the region, these enchanting tales are sure to be enjoyed and shared time and again.

ISBN 978 0 7509 6138 7

Visit our website and discover thousands of other History Press books.

www.thehistorypress.co.uk

CW00546125
How a Realist Hero
Rebuilt the Kingdom
Manga ✠ Satoshi Ueda
Original Work ✠ Dojyomaru
Original Character Design ✠ Fuyuyuki

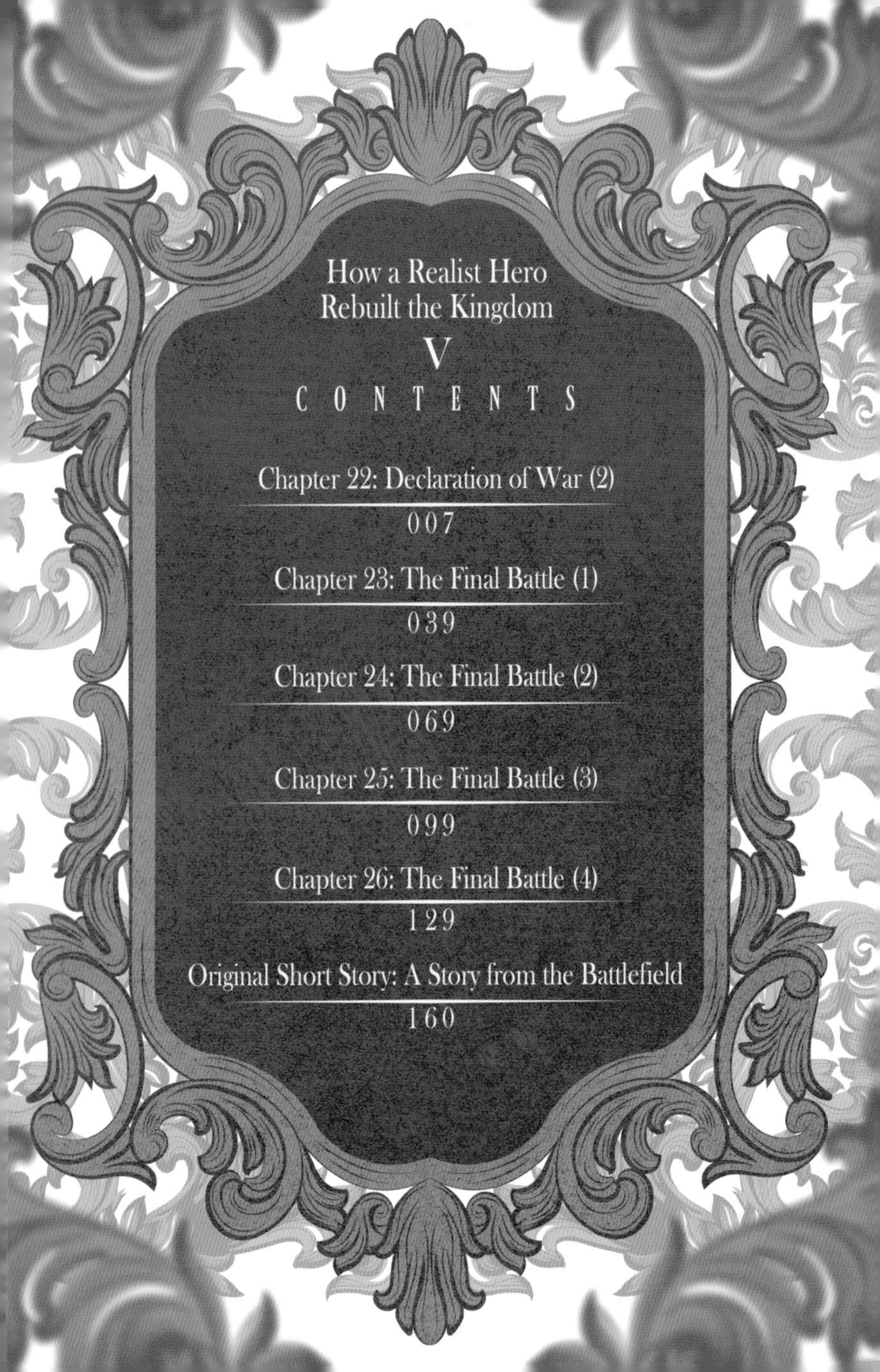

How a Realist Hero
Rebuilt the Kingdom

V

CONTENTS

Chapter 22: Declaration of War (2)
007

Chapter 23: The Final Battle (1)
039

Chapter 24: The Final Battle (2)
069

Chapter 25: The Final Battle (3)
099

Chapter 26: The Final Battle (4)
129

Original Short Story: A Story from the Battlefield
160